US
Government Corruption

Other Books in the Current Controversies Series

US
Government Corruption

Debra A. Miller, Book Editor

GREENHAVEN PRESS
A part of Gale, Cengage Learning

Detroit • New York • San Francisco • New Haven, Conn • Waterville, Maine • London

Elizabeth Des Chenes, *Managing Editor*

© 2012 Greenhaven Press, a part of Gale, Cengage Learning

Gale and Greenhaven Press are registered trademarks used herein under license.

For more information, contact:
Greenhaven Press
27500 Drake Rd.
Farmington Hills, MI 48331-3535
Or you can visit our Internet site at gale.cengage.com

For product information and technology assistance, contact us at

Gale Customer Support, 1-800-877-4253
For permission to use material from this text or product, submit all requests online at www.cengage.com/permissions

Further permissions questions can be emailed to permissionrequest@cengage.com

Articles in Greenhaven Press anthologies are often edited for length to meet page requirements. In addition, original titles of these works are changed to clearly present the main thesis and to explicitly indicate the author's opinion. Every effort is made to ensure that Greenhaven Press accurately reflects the original intent of the authors. Every effort has been made to trace the owners of copyrighted material.

Cover image copyright © Tetra Images/Corbis.

LIBRARY OF CONGRESS CATALOGING-IN-PUBLICATION DATA

US government corruption / Debra A. Miller, book editor.
    p. cm. -- (Current controversies)
    Includes bibliographical references and index.
    ISBN 978-0-7377-5622-7 (hbk.) -- ISBN 978-0-7377-5623-4 (pbk.)
    1. Political corruption--United States. 2. Corruption--United States. I. Miller, Debra A. II. Title: United States government corruption.
    JK2249.U75 2011
    364.1'3230973--dc22

                                                                    2011008704

Printed in the United States of America
1 2 3 4 5 6 7 15 14 13 12 11

Contents

The Supreme Court in *Citizens United v. Federal Election Commission* did not eliminate all campaign finance restrictions on corporations. Corporations and unions are still prohibited from making direct contributions to candidates in federal elections. In addition, the Court also upheld disclaimer and disclosure requirements in federal campaign finance laws.

Chapter 2: Is Corruption Destroying the US Financial System?

Chapter 4: What Are the Remedies for US Government Corruption?

Foreword

By definition, controversies are "discussions of questions in which opposing opinions clash" (Webster's Twentieth Century Dictionary Unabridged). Few would deny that controversies are a pervasive part of the human condition and exist on virtually every level of human enterprise. Controversies transpire between individuals and among groups, within nations and between nations. Controversies supply the grist necessary for progress by providing challenges and challengers to the status quo. They also create atmospheres where strife and warfare can flourish. A world without controversies would be a peaceful world; but it also would be, by and large, static and prosaic.

The Series' Purpose

The purpose of the Current Controversies series is to explore many of the social, political, and economic controversies dominating the national and international scenes today. Titles selected for inclusion in the series are highly focused and specific. For example, from the larger category of criminal justice, Current Controversies deals with specific topics such as police brutality, gun control, white collar crime, and others. The debates in Current Controversies also are presented in a useful, timeless fashion. Articles and book excerpts included in each title are selected if they contribute valuable, long-range ideas to the overall debate. And wherever possible, current information is enhanced with historical documents and other relevant materials. Thus, while individual titles are current in focus, every effort is made to ensure that they will not become quickly outdated. Books in the Current Controversies series will remain important resources for librarians, teachers, and students for many years.

In addition to keeping the titles focused and specific, great care is taken in the editorial format of each book in the series. Book introductions and chapter prefaces are offered to provide background material for readers. Chapters are organized around several key questions that are answered with diverse opinions representing all points on the political spectrum. Materials in each chapter include opinions in which authors clearly disagree as well as alternative opinions in which authors may agree on a broader issue but disagree on the possible solutions. In this way, the content of each volume in Current Controversies mirrors the mosaic of opinions encountered in society. Readers will quickly realize that there are many viable answers to these complex issues. By questioning each author's conclusions, students and casual readers can begin to develop the critical thinking skills so important to evaluating opinionated material.

Current Controversies is also ideal for controlled research. Each anthology in the series is composed of primary sources taken from a wide gamut of informational categories including periodicals, newspapers, books, US and foreign government documents, and the publications of private and public organizations. Readers will find factual support for reports, debates, and research papers covering all areas of important issues. In addition, an annotated table of contents, an index, a book and periodical bibliography, and a list of organizations to contact are included in each book to expedite further research.

Perhaps more than ever before in history, people are confronted with diverse and contradictory information. During the Persian Gulf War, for example, the public was not only treated to minute-to-minute coverage of the war, it was also inundated with critiques of the coverage and countless analyses of the factors motivating US involvement. Being able to sort through the plethora of opinions accompanying today's major issues, and to draw one's own conclusions, can be a complicated and frustrating struggle. It is the editors' hope that Current Controversies will help readers with this struggle.

Introduction

> *"Commentators often describe today's campaign finance situation in the United States as 'legal corruption' because it allows private interests to buy access to and influence with government officials in a way that is technically legal under existing laws."*

Government corruption, broadly speaking, occurs whenever political leaders, elected officials, or other government actors subvert the central purpose of government—which is to promote the public good—for private benefit. The definition of corruption used by the World Bank and the International Monetary Fund (IMF), for example, is "the abuse of public office for private gain." According to most experts in this field, corruption can take various forms—everything from illegal bribes or kickbacks to government officials, to conflicts of interests or ethical violations affecting government work, to more systemic but often legal types of corruption such as the campaign finance and lobbying scandals often featured in US news reports. Many experts conclude that all forms of corruption, whether illegal or legal, pose a threat to democratic principles.

Direct Types of Corruption

The most blatant, but probably least common, types of corruption affecting the US government are clear quid pro quo (something for something) actions such as bribery (the giving of gifts to government officials in return for a government action); graft (the use of government expertise for self-enrichment); and extortion (the illegal use of one's official position to obtain property, funds, or other benefit). Other forms of direct corruption include nepotism (favoring friends or relatives for government jobs), fraud (deception for personal gain), embezzlement (stealing government funds or property), and influence peddling (using influence with government officials to obtain favors for another person, usually for payment.)

In many cases, the motivation for these types of corruption is some form of private financial gain. The scandal involving former California Republican congressman Randy "Duke" Cunningham illustrates this point. Cunningham used his position on the House intelligence and appropriations committees to steer millions of dollars in government contracts to defense firms in exchange for $2.4 million in bribes. The bribes included purchase of Cunningham's San Diego house at an inflated price, a forty-two-foot yacht, $1 million in checks, a $200,000 down payment on a condominium, and numerous other lavish gifts. In December 2005 Cunningham pled guilty to bribery and tax evasion; he is serving an eight-year prison term.

In some cases, however, the motivation is not money, but power. The 1970s political scandal known as Watergate provides an example of this type of corruption. Questions first arose when burglars were caught breaking into Democratic Party offices in a Washington, DC, office building. As the facts unraveled, the public learned that the scandal involved a slush fund of secret, illegal corporate donations maintained by US president Richard Nixon, a Republican—monies that were used to spy on and discredit the president's political enemies. In the United States, these types of corruption are illegal, subject to various laws intended to root out corruption in government.

Corporate Campaign Contributions and Corruption

In democracies like the United States, however, experts say that the most worrisome types of corruption tend to involve much more subtle, often legal practices, most notably claims of influence buying in the financing of political campaigns. Concerns about campaign finance have risen along with the spiraling costs of running a campaign for federal elected office. The parties willing to contribute large amounts to fund political ads or campaigns tend to be corporations, unions, or special interest groups that have both significant resources and specific political agendas they wish to promote. Although there is rarely any proof that candidates promise votes as payment for campaign contributions or assistance, critics argue that politicians become indebted to their funding sources for campaign funds and are thus inclined to act in favor of these private interests rather than in the public interest when legislating or formulating government policies.

Numerous campaign finance reforms have been enacted over the years to try to regulate and disclose campaign contributions, but loopholes are always found to allow legal requirements and prohibitions to be circumvented. The result is that corporations, unions, and other private entities are able to plow ever larger amounts of cash into US congressional and presidential elections, dwarfing the monies that can be raised from ordinary, individual citizens. Many critics say that a 2010 US Supreme Court decision, *Citizens United v. Federal Election Commission*, has opened the floodgates to even more corporate participation in elections by holding that the First Amendment free speech guarantee prohibits Congress from barring corporations from spending funds to support or oppose political candidates. Commentators often describe today's campaign finance situation in the United States as "legal corruption" because it allows private interests to buy access to and influence with government officials in a way that is technically legal under existing laws.

Lobbying and Corruption

Another type of activity often viewed as legal corruption in the United States involves the use of high-paid professional lobbyists by corporations and interest groups. One concern about lobbying involves the large amounts spent on lobbying by private interests who also often make campaign contributions. Although there is rarely a clear quid pro quo, critics charge that elected officials often implicitly understand that they are expected to favor the interests that funded their campaigns. Legislators who defy this implicit agreement risk losing campaign support needed for reelection. Additional problems of corruption involve the so-called "revolving door" practice of politicians being hired as lobbyists and lobbyists being hired or appointed to government jobs. This gives private interests inside knowledge and contacts to influence legislation or government decisions—access that ordinary citizens seldom have. Many commentators have noted in recent years, for example, that Wall Street insiders have moved in and out of government, often acquiring appointments to powerful government positions that allow them to influence national economic policies. Like campaign contributions, this use of professional lobbyists is not illegal, although lobbyists are prohibited from directly bribing legislators with money or gifts and are required to register with the government and comply with certain disclosure requirements.

The Threat to Democracy

Critics claim that this system of campaign finance and lobbying in the United States produces a Congress and a government that is more accountable to corporate and special interests than to the public interest—the basic recipe for corruption. This corruption, critics say, destroys the public's trust in government because it violates the basic democratic principle that government must be representative of the people and work for the public good. Many commentators see this phenomenon already happening in the United States, as revealed in public opinion polls about the public's declining trust in Congress and as shown in the 2010 midterm congressional elections, in which voters in many states threw out incumbents and elected novice senators and representatives, many of them members of the Tea Party, a grassroots citizens group.

The viewpoints contained in *Current Controversies: US Government Corruption* address the issue of government corruption in the United States. The authors included in this volume discuss just how serious US government corruption is, whether it is destroying the US financial system, whether the *Citizens United* decision will lead to more corruption, and what the possible remedies are for corruption.

How Serious Is Government Corruption in the United States?

Chapter Preface

Unlike some developing nations, the United States has some of the toughest anticorruption laws in the world. US law has contained prohibitions against bribery, for example, since the nation's founding. In fact, the US Constitution, article 2, section 4 provides: "The President, Vice President and all civil Officers of the United States, shall be removed from Office on Impeachment for, and Conviction of, Treason, Bribery, or other high Crimes and Misdemeanors." Today, various types of political bribery and influence are also considered to be criminal offenses under US federal statutes. Other federal laws regulate campaign contributions. Yet, according to many legal and political analysts, these laws have been interpreted in ways that make it difficult to prosecute corruption and that allow activities that other developed nations would consider to be corrupt.

The Bribery Act

The main US law prohibiting corruption is the Bribery Act, a law enacted in 1962 to prohibit corruption among officials of the federal government. The act applies to a wide range of federal officials including those who work in the judicial, executive, and legislative branches; private citizens who work for organizations that receive funds from the federal government; witnesses in various kinds of federal proceedings; and federal jurors. Section 201 of the act makes it a crime for federal officials to accept, or for anyone to give, a bribe or an official gratuity. Both offenses require proof that something of value was requested, offered, or given to the federal official. However, the offense of bribery requires that something of value be given in exchange for influence over an official act and that this be given or received with corrupt intent. The offense of giving a gratuity simply requires that something was given for or because of an official act. Bribery is punishable by up to fifteen years in prison, whereas the less serious offense of payment or receipt of an official gratuity is punishable by up to two years in prison and a fine. The Bribery Act does not apply to state and local officials or to employees of private firms; various other federal and state corruption provisions cover these individuals.

Because the language of the Bribery Act is relatively broad and could cover a wide range of inconsequential activities, federal courts have provided some guidelines to limit its application. In *United States v. Sun-Diamond Growers of California* (1999), for example, the US Supreme Court limited the Bribery Act substantially. This case involved an agricultural trade association that lobbied federal agencies and officials, often wining and dining these federal officials in the hopes that they might consider the association's interests when issuing regulations or making other government decisions. In *Sun-Diamond*, Secretary of Agriculture Mike Espy was the federal official who received the association's gifts, which included tickets to a tennis tournament and several expensive meals. The trial court convicted the association of giving illegal gratuities, but the Supreme Court ruled that it is not an illegal gratuity for gifts to be given to a federal official just to build up a reservoir of goodwill, as long as the gifts were not given to influence a particular matter being decided by the official.

In *Sun-Diamond*, the Court thus made prosecution of crimes under the Bribery Act much more difficult and sanctioned a wide range of lobbying activities that many people might view as corrupt. To remedy this situation, some members of Congress have pressed for legislation to toughen the Bribery Act. The latest such effort was the Public Corruption Prosecution Improvements Act of 2009 (PCPIA)—a bill introduced in the Senate by Senator Patrick Leahy (D-VT) to strengthen federal criminal laws on corruption by addressing the various narrow court interpretations of the Bribery Act. However, neither this bill nor any similar legislation has been enacted into law.

Nevertheless, the Bribery Act has been used successfully to fight government corruption. The most recent example came in the form of a United States Federal Bureau of Investigation (FBI) sting operation called Abscam, in which FBI agents set up a fictitious company, Abdul Enterprises, to lure various public officials into accepting bribes. In the late 1970s and 1980s, FBI agents secretly videotaped meetings between various high-ranking federal and state officials and a man posing as an Arab sheik seeking various official favors. The investigation ultimately led to the conviction of one US senator and five members of the US House of Representatives for bribery. Four state and local government officials were also convicted, as well as an inspector for the US Immigration and Naturalization Service.

Campaign Finance Laws

A second major focus of US anticorruption laws has been in the area of campaign finance. Early in the nation's history, it was routine for wealthy speculators and entrepreneurs to pour large amounts of money into politics to buy votes and political influence, and a series of important reforms were passed in the early part of the twentieth century to address this problem. One of the first significant reforms, for example, was the 1907 Tillman Act, a law that prohibited corporations and national banks from contributing to federal campaigns. The most sweeping campaign finance laws, however, were passed in the wake of Watergate—a notorious political scandal that erupted in 1972 and eventually lead to the resignation of US president Richard Nixon—as well as in recent years. Like the Bribery Act, however, federal campaign finance laws have been weakened by federal court decisions.

The first modern campaign finance law was the 1971 Federal Election Campaign Act (FECA), which required candidates for federal office to disclose sources of campaign contributions and campaign expenditures. Following the Watergate scandal, however, Congress virtually rewrote the original FECA law by passing amendments in 1974. The amended FECA helped to create the first program of public campaign funding for presidential elections, strengthened disclosure provisions, and set strict new limits on campaign contributions and expenditures. To enforce these provisions, the law created a new federal agency—the Federal Election Commission (FEC).

However, in 1976, the US Supreme Court ruled many parts of the new FECA unconstitutional for violating the First Amendment to the US Constitution. In the landmark case *Buckley v. Valeo*, the Court held that the act of spending money for political campaigns was entitled to constitutional free speech protections as long as the entity spending the money did not coordinate directly with campaigns or use any of a list of words that the Court said would constitute "express" advocacy on behalf of or against a candidate (such as "vote for," "elect," or "defeat"). The decision thus eliminated all of FECA's limits on so-called independent campaign expenditures, such as advertising by political action committees (PACs). According to many experts, the decision unleashed a new wave of cash into American elections in the form of issue ads paid for by PACs. In addition, loopholes in the law were later found to allow corporations to contribute directly to campaigns in the form of "bundled" employee contributions and so-called "soft money" (unregulated funds) collected and spent by political parties.

To curb the use of these loopholes, Congress eventually passed the Bipartisan Campaign Reform Act of 2002 (BCRA, also known as "McCain-Feingold" after its Senate sponsors). The BCRA prohibited corporations from making contributions to national political parties (called "soft money"), and provided that political issue ads that refer to a federal candidate could not be broadcast within thirty days of a primary and sixty days of an election. Wealthy donors and corporations, however, soon circumvented this law, too, by using tax-exempt political organizations known as 527 groups, which are not regulated by the FEC, to fund issue ads.

According to many political experts, the final blow to effective campaign finance regulation came in early 2010, when the US Supreme Court ruled in *Citizens United v. Federal Election Commission* that corporate funding of independent issue ads cannot be limited in any way because such a ban violates corporations' right to free speech under the First Amendment to the Constitution. Although corporations are still prohibited from making direct contributions to candidates, they are now permitted to spend unlimited amounts on political ads supporting or opposing candidates for federal office—a distinction that critics say is almost irrelevant.

The viewpoints in this chapter present a range of views about the role of money in elections and whether corporations have a corrupting influence on US government.

America's Democracy Is Now Fundamentally Corrupted

Lawrence Lessig

Lawrence Lessig is a professor of law at Harvard Law School and cofounder of the nonprofit Change Congress, a nonpartisan advocacy organization that seeks to protect the independence of Congress by fighting the influence of money in politics.

We should remember what it felt like one year ago [February 2009], as the ability to recall it emotionally will pass and it is an emotional memory as much as anything else. It was a moment rare in a democracy's history. The feeling was palpable—to supporters and opponents alike—that something important had happened. America had elected, the young candidate [Barack Obama] promised, a transformational president. And wrapped in a campaign that had produced the biggest influx of new voters and small-dollar contributions in a generation, the claim seemed credible, almost intoxicating, and just in time.

Yet a year into the presidency of Barack Obama, it is already clear that this administration is an opportunity missed. Not because it is too conservative. Not because it is too liberal. But because it is too conventional. Obama has given up the rhetoric of his early campaign—a campaign that promised to "challenge the broken system in Washington" and to "fundamentally change the way Washington works." Indeed, "fundamental change" is no longer even a hint. . . .

A Corrupt Congress

At the center of our government lies a bankrupt institution: Congress. Not financially bankrupt, at least not yet, but politically bankrupt. *Bush v. Gore* notwithstanding, Americans' faith

Lawrence Lessig, "How to Get Our Democracy Back," *The Nation*, February 3, 2010. TheNation.com. Reproduced by permission.

in the Supreme Court remains extraordinarily high—76 percent have a fair or great deal of "trust and confidence" in the Court. Their faith in the presidency is also high—61 percent.

This is corruption. Not the corruption of bribes. . . . [but] a corruption of the faith Americans have in this core institution of our democracy.

But consistently and increasingly over the past decade, faith in Congress has collapsed—slowly, and then all at once. Today it is at a record low. Just 45 percent of Americans have "trust and confidence" in Congress; just 25 percent approve of how Congress is handling its job. A higher percentage of Americans likely supported the British Crown at the time of the Revolution than support our Congress today.

The source of America's cynicism is not hard to find. Americans despise the inauthentic. Gregory House, of the eponymous TV medical drama [*House*], is a hero not because he is nice (he isn't) but because he is true. Tiger Woods is a disappointment not because he is evil (he isn't) but because he proved false. We may want peace and prosperity, but most would settle for simple integrity. Yet the single attribute least attributed to Congress, at least in the minds of the vast majority of Americans, is just that: integrity. And this is because most believe our Congress is a simple pretense. That rather than being, as our framers promised, an institution "dependent on the People," the institution has developed a pathological dependence on campaign cash. The US Congress has become the Fund-Raising Congress. And it answers—as Republican and Democratic presidents alike have discovered—not to the people, and not even to the president, but increasingly to the relatively small mix of interests that fund the key races that determine which party will be in power.

This is corruption. Not the corruption of bribes, or of any other crime known to Title 18 of the US Code. Instead, it is a corruption of the faith Americans have in this core institution of our democracy. The vast majority of Americans believe money buys results in Congress (88 percent in a recent California poll). And whether that belief is true or not, the damage is the same. The democracy is feigned. A feigned democracy breeds cynicism. Cynicism leads to disengagement. Disengagement leaves the fox guarding the henhouse.

In Plain Sight

This corruption is not hidden. On the contrary, it is in plain sight, with its practices simply more and more brazen. Consider, for example, the story [author] Robert [G.] Kaiser tells in his fantastic book *So Damn Much Money*, about Senator John Stennis, who served for forty-one years until his retirement in 1989. Stennis, no choirboy himself, was asked by a colleague to host a fund-raiser for military contractors while he was chair of the Armed Services Committee. "Would that be proper?" Stennis asked. "I hold life and death over those companies. I don't think it would be proper for me to take money from them."

Is such a norm even imaginable in DC today? Compare Stennis with Max Baucus, who has gladly opened his campaign chest to $3.3 million in contributions from the health care and insurance industries since 2005, a time when he has controlled health care in the Senate. Or Senators [Joseph] Lieberman, [Evan] Bayh and [Ben] Nelson, who took millions from insurance and health care interests and then opposed the (in their states) popular public option for health care. Or any number of Blue Dog Democrats [moderates] in the House who did the same, including, most prominently, Arkansas's Mike Ross. Or Republican John Campbell, a California landlord who in 2008 received (as ethics reports indicate) between $600,000 and $6 million in rent from used car dealers, who successfully inserted an amendment into the Consumer Financial Protection Agency Act to exempt car dealers from financing rules to protect consumers. Or Democrats Melissa Bean and Walter Minnick, who took top-dollar contributions from the financial services sector and then opposed stronger oversight of financial regulations.

The list is endless; the practice open and notorious. Since the time of Rome, historians have taught that while corruption is a part of every society, the only truly dangerous corruption comes when the society has lost any sense of shame. Washington has lost its sense of shame.

Getting Rich in Politics

As fund-raising becomes the focus of Congress—as the parties force members to raise money for other members, as they reward the best fund-raisers with lucrative committee assignments and leadership positions—the focus of congressional "work" shifts. Like addicts constantly on the lookout for their next fix, members grow impatient with anything that doesn't promise the kick of a campaign contribution. The first job is meeting the fund-raising target. Everything else seems cheap. Talk about policy becomes, as one Silicon Valley executive described it to me, "transactional." The perception, at least among industry staffers dealing with the Hill, is that one makes policy progress only if one can promise fund-raising progress as well.

This dance has in turn changed the character of Washington. As Kaiser explains, Joe Rothstein, an aide to former Senator Mike Gravel, said there was never a "period of pristine American politics untainted by money. . . . Money has been part of American politics forever, on occasion—in the Gilded Age or the [Warren G.] Harding administration, for example—much more blatantly than recently." But "in recent decades 'the scale of it has just gotten way out of hand.' The money may have come in brown paper bags in earlier eras, but the politicians needed, and took, much less of it than they take through more formal channels today."

And not surprisingly, as powerful interests from across the nation increasingly invest in purchasing public policy rather than inventing a better mousetrap, wealth, and a certain class of people, shift to Washington. According to the 2000 Census, fourteen of the hundred richest counties were in the Washington area. In 2007, nine of the richest twenty were in the area. Again, Kaiser: "In earlier generations enterprising young men came to Washington looking for power and political adventure, often with ambitions to save or reform the country or the world. In the last fourth of the twentieth century such aspirations were supplanted by another familiar American yearning: to get rich."

Rich, indeed, they are, with the godfather of the lobbyist class, Gerald Cassidy, amassing more than $100 million from his lobbying business.

If money really doesn't affect results in Washington, then what could possibly explain the fundamental policy failures . . . of our government over the past decades?

The Effect of Money in Politics

Members of Congress are insulted by charges like these. They insist that money has no such effect. Perhaps, they concede, it buys access. (As former Representative Romano Mazzoli put it, "People who contribute get the ear of the member and the ear of the staff. They have the access—and access is it.") But, the cash seekers insist, it doesn't change anyone's mind. The souls of members are not corrupted by private funding. It is simply the way Americans go about raising the money necessary to elect our government. . . .

Here a second and completely damning response walks onto the field, if money really doesn't affect results in Washington, then what could possibly explain the fundamental policy failures—relative to every comparable democracy across the world, whether liberal or conservative—of our government over the past decades? The choice (made by Democrats and Republicans alike) to leave unchecked a huge and crucially vulnerable segment of our economy, which threw the economy over a cliff when it tanked (as independent analysts again and again predicted it would). Or the choice to leave unchecked the spread of greenhouse gases. Or to leave unregulated the exploding use of antibiotics in our food supply—producing deadly strains of *E. coli*. Or the inability of the twenty years of "small government" Republican presidents in the past twenty-nine to reduce the size of government at all. Or . . . you fill in the blank. From the perspective of what the people want, or even the perspective of what the political parties say they want, the Fund-Raising Congress is misfiring in every dimension. That is either because Congress is filled with idiots or because Congress has a dependency on something other than principle or public policy sense. In my view, Congress is not filled with idiots.

A Corruption of Democracy

The point is simple, if extraordinarily difficult for those of us proud of our traditions to accept: This democracy no longer works. Its central player has been captured. Corrupted. Controlled by an economy of influence disconnected from the democracy. Congress has developed a dependency foreign to the framers' design. Corporate campaign spending, now liberated by the Supreme Court [in the 2010 ruling in *Citizens United v. Federal Election Commission*], will only make that dependency worse. "A dependence" not, as the Federalist Papers celebrated it, "on the People" but a dependency upon interests that have conspired to produce a world in which policy gets sold. . . .

Obama's Failure

A year into this administration, it is impossible to believe [that changing the corrupted machinery of government] is anywhere on the administration's radar, at least anymore. The need to reform Congress has left Obama's rhetoric. The race to dicker with Congress in the same way Congress always deals is now the plan. Symbolic limits on lobbyists within the administration and calls for new disclosure limits for Congress are the sole tickets of "reform." (Even its revolving door policy left a Mack truck-wide gap at its core: Members of the administration can't leave the government and lobby for the industries they regulated during the term of the administration. But the day after Obama leaves office? All bets are off.) Save a vague promise in his State of the Union about overturning the Court's decision in *Citizens United v. Federal Election Commission* (as if that were reform enough), there is nothing in the current framework of the White House's plans that is anything more than the strategy of a kinder and gentler, albeit certainly more articulate, George W. Bush: buying reform at whatever price the Fund-Raising Congress demands. No doubt Obama will try to buy more reform than Bush did. But the terms will continue to be set by a Congress driven by a dependency that betrays democracy, and at a price that is not clear we can even afford.

Health care reform is a perfect example. The bill the Fund-Raising Congress has produced is miles from the reform that Obama promised ("Any plan I sign must include an insurance exchange . . . including a public option," July 19, 2009). Like the stimulus package, like the bank bailouts, it is larded with gifts to the most powerful fund-raising interests—including a promise to drug companies to pay retail prices for wholesale purchases and a promise to the insurance companies to leave their effectively collusive (since exempt from antitrust limitations) and extraordinarily inefficient system of insurance intact—and provides (relative to the promises) little to the supposed intended beneficiaries of the law: the uninsured. In this, it is the perfect complement to the only significant social legislation enacted by Bush, the prescription drug benefit: a small benefit to those who can't afford drugs, a big gift to those who make drugs and an astonishingly expensive price tag for the nation.

So how did Obama get to this sorry bill? The first step, we are told, was to sit down with representatives from the insurance and pharmaceutical industries to work out a deal. But why, the student of Obama's campaign might ask, were they the entities with whom to strike a deal? How many of the 69,498,516 votes received by Obama did they actually cast? "We have to change our politics," Obama said. Where is the change in this?

"People . . . watch," Obama told us in the campaign, "as every year, candidates offer up detailed health care plans with great fanfare and promise, only to see them crushed under the weight of Washington politics and drug and insurance industry lobbying once the campaign is over."

"This cannot," he said, "be one of those years."

It has been one of those years. And it will continue to be so long as presidents continue to give a free pass to the underlying corruption of our democracy: Congress.

There was a way Obama might have had this differently. It would have been risky, some might say audacious. And it would have required an imagination far beyond the conventional politics that now controls his administration.

No doubt, 2009 was going to be an extraordinarily difficult year. Our nation was a cancer patient hit by a bus on her way to begin chemotherapy. The first stages of reform thus had to be trauma care, at least to stabilize the patient until more fundamental treatment could begin.

But even then, there was an obvious way that Obama could have reserved the recognition of the need for this more fundamental reform by setting up the expectations of the nation forcefully and clearly. Building on the rhetoric at the core of his campaign, on January 20, 2009, Obama could have said:

America has spoken. It has demanded a fundamental change in how Washington works, and in the government America delivers. I commit to America to work with Congress to produce that change. But if we fail, if Congress blocks the change that America has demanded—or more precisely, if Congress allows the special interests that control it to block the change that America has demanded—then it will be time to remake Congress. Not by throwing out the Democrats, or by throwing out the Republicans. But by throwing out both, to the extent that both continue to want to work in the old way. If this Congress fails to deliver change, then we will change Congress.

Had he framed his administration in these terms, then when what has happened happened, Obama would be holding the means to bring about the obvious and critical transformation that our government requires: an end to the Fund-Raising Congress. The failure to deliver on the promises of the campaign would not be the failure of Obama to woo Republicans (the unwooable Victorians of our age). The failure would have been what America was already primed to believe: a failure of this corrupted institution to do its job. Once that failure was marked with a frame that Obama set, he would have been in the position to begin the extraordinarily difficult campaign to effect the real change that Congress needs.

I am not saying this would have been easy. It wouldn't have. It would have been the most important constitutional struggle since the New Deal or the Civil War. It would have involved a fundamental remaking of the way Congress works. No one should minimize how hard that would have been. But if there was a president who could have done this, it was, in my view, Obama. No politician in almost a century has had the demonstrated capacity to inspire the imagination of a nation. He had us, all of us, and could have kept us had he kept the focus high.

Political Corruption Played a Large Role in Health Care Reform

Jonathan Weiler

Jonathan Weiler is a professor of international studies at the University of North Carolina at Chapel Hill and co-author of the book Authoritarianism and Polarization in Contemporary American Politics.

Editor's note: The public option was, indeed, dropped and was not included in the health care bill that passed the Congress in 2010.

For decades now, American political leaders, as well as global financial institutions, like the World Bank and the IMF [International Monetary Fund], have lectured to poorer countries about the need to root out corruption. A system or government compromised by insiderism, favoritism and lack of transparency will fail to establish the foundations for sustained prosperity and, in the process, weaken the kind of accountability and fealty to the rule of law necessary for democratic governance in the public interest. Thus the sometimes "tough medicine" that the IMF and World Bank prescribed to developing countries, backed by the United States, included a strong dose of anticorruption efforts in support of good governance.

Corruption in Health Care Reform

So it's worth pointing out that corruption—presumed to have been confined in American history to our Tammany-Hall past [a reference to a Democratic political machine that controlled politics in New York City in the 1800s and early 1900s]—is an

Jonathan Weiler, "Health Care Reform and Corruption," *The Huffington Post*, October 1, 2009. HuffingtonPost.com. Reproduced by permission.

endemic feature of our own political system. It's played an important role, for example, in the current health care reform debate. Let's leave aside the very questionable and secretive deal that the White House made with the pharmaceutical industry and just focus on the public option [a proposal for government-run health care]. Polls that clearly define the public option show that large majorities of Americans support it. The quality of arguments against the public option (setting aside "death panel" garbage)—for example, that it's "unfair" because a publicly run health insurance option would be cheaper and be run more efficiently than is private insurance—is, frankly, pathetic. And yet, despite a Democratic super majority in the Senate, the public option appears headed for defeat. Why? In large part because key Democrats are carrying water for the health industry interests that line their pockets. As [writer] Nate Silver has shown, you can, in fact, explain quite well whether, for example, so-called moderate Senators will support the public option if you know how much they've received in contributions from health industry PACs [political action committees]. Yes, this is perfectly legal. But, in any other context, we'd call a legislative process so clearly infected by moneyed interests what it is: corrupt.

As [Nobel Prize–winning economist Paul] Krugman recently observed, in a column waxing nostalgic (to a point) for President [Richard] Nixon:

> We tend to think of the way things are now, with a huge army of lobbyists permanently camped in the corridors of power, with corporations prepared to unleash misleading ads and organize fake grassroots protests against any legislation that threatens their bottom line, as the way it always was. But our corporate-cash-dominated system is a relatively recent creation, dating mainly from the late 1970s.

> And now that this system exists, reform of any kind has become extremely difficult. That's especially true for health care, where growing spending has made the vested interests

far more powerful than they were in Nixon's day. The health insurance industry, in particular, saw its premiums go from 1.5 percent of GDP [gross domestic product, a measure of the country's economic output] in 1970 to 5.5 percent in 2007, so that a once minor player has become a political behemoth, one that is currently spending $1.4 million a day lobbying Congress.

That spending fuels debates that otherwise seem incomprehensible. Why are "centrist" Democrats like Senator Kent Conrad of North Dakota so opposed to letting a public plan, in which Americans can buy their insurance directly from the government, compete with private insurers? Never mind their often incoherent arguments; what it comes down to is the money.

And such influence also obstructs serious reform efforts that might not include a public option. [Author and journalist] Jonathan Cohn has explained that the health insurance system in the Netherlands relies mainly on private health insurance that includes for-profit providers. And that system is highly successful—universal coverage, comprehensive care, high levels of satisfaction and excellent outcomes. But Cohn also points out one key ingredient in the Dutch system that makes it unlikely to serve as a viable model for the United States: stringent government regulation and oversight.

Cohn writes:

Still, there's a catch. A big catch. Private insurance in the Netherlands works because it operates more or less like a public utility. The Dutch government regulates industry practices tightly—more tightly than the reforms now moving through Congress propose to do in the United States. The public insurance option was supposed to make up for that deficiency, at least in part, by setting a standard for service and affordability that the private industry would have to meet—and by offering a fail-safe option in case the private plans simply couldn't keep up. If Congress ends up gutting the public plan, in part or in whole, then it needs to work even harder on making private insurance work. And it's an open question whether that will happen.

It's an open question (to put it optimistically) because of the way our legislative processes are compromised. In short, because of corruption.

Widespread Corruption

Of course, it's not just health reform. There have been a spate of stories in recent days—from malfeasance among defense contractors (brought to light anew by that ridiculous bill to de-fund ACORN [Association of Community Organizers for Reform Now]), to successful financial industry efforts to undermine consumer-friendly banking regulations, to politically pressured FDA [Federal Drug Administration] approval of dangerous medical devices—that highlight how widespread corruption is in our political system.

Earlier this year [2009], Simon Johnson, the former chief economist of the International Monetary Fund, wrote a widely discussed article, "The Quiet Coup," about the degree to which the American financial system had come to embody the practices we typically associate with corrupt "emerging market" economies, like Russia. Central to such practices included the capacity of powerful private interests—including those most responsible for economic crisis and instability—to block changes to a status quo that served their narrow purposes at the expense of the public interest. This kind of skewed outcome is at the heart of what is so pernicious about corruption. And it appears, increasingly, to pervade our political system, calling into question, among other things, our credibility in lecturing to the rest of the world about good governance.

Physician, heal thyself.

Government Corruption in America Is on the Rise

Joseph Schuman

Joseph Schuman is a senior correspondent for AolNews.com.

Is corruption getting worse in the United States?

That may seem the takeaway from this year's [2010's] Corruption Perceptions Index from Berlin-based Transparency International, which saw the U.S. 2010 ranking slip to 22nd out of 178 nations from 19th last year—the first time the United States has missed inclusion in the top 20 least-corrupt countries since the index was launched 15 years ago.

Rising past the U.S. over the year were the tiny Caribbean island nation of Barbados (now 17th), the Persian Gulf emirate Qatar (19th) and Chile (21st). New Zealand, Denmark and Singapore—ranked Nos. 1, 2 and 3 last year—tied for first place in 2010.

US Corruption and the Financial Crisis

At 22nd, the U.S. is now tied with Belgium, a country known among fellow Western Europeans for a dysfunctional political system that has been unable to produce a governing coalition since April, and took more than nine months to do so after the last election in March 2007.

But this isn't because Americans are more subject to rampant bribery, extortionate government contract practices or the host of crooked schemes that affect personal and public life on a daily basis in much of the world. (Three-quarters of the 178 nations in the index scored below five on a scale of one to 10, with 10 being the cleanest. The U.S. score was 7.1, down from 7.5 last year.)

Rather, the worsening perception of U.S. corruption seems due to the financial crisis that has shaken American lives, meshed with financial scandals that have dominated headlines over the past decade.

"When you think about the last several years, there have been running trends, scandals like Enron and WorldCom, Bernie Madoff . . . a wide variety of scandals that are both illegal, corrupt in the legal sense, and corrupt legal acts," said Nancy Boswell, the president of Transparency International-USA. "There has been a general sense coming out of the crisis that people have lost their jobs, are underwater on mortgages. Maybe some of what went on is legal, but it seems like ethics and integrity took a back seat."

Transparency International, a global network of groups that doesn't investigate alleged corruption but works with organizations that do and campaigns for tougher laws and enforcement, compiles its index from surveys conducted by international nongovernmental organizations like the World Bank and private research from the likes of the Economist Intelligence Unit and the World Economic Forum.

It defines corruption as "the abuse of entrusted power for private gain."

By that standard, the past year of headline-making investigations into Wall Street practices and associated government lapses has brought to light a narrative of unbridled greed that has undermined confidence in public institutions and stoked perceptions of corruption here.

Money in Politics

Another factor, Boswell noted, is the increasingly unrestrained and covert role of private money in the political system—especially since the Supreme Court's *Citizens United [v. Federal Election Commission]* decision in January [2010], which former Justice Sandra Day O'Connor criticized as a threat to judicial independence and checks on campaign spending.

"There is a perception in the American public that the system is broken," Boswell said. "There's no one reason, but there's a myriad of reasons that come together."

Perceptions of Corruption

Transparency International uses the perception index because corruption "is to a great extent a hidden activity that is difficult to measure," the group said. "Over time, perceptions have proved to be a reliable estimate of corruption. Measuring scandals, investigations or prosecutions, while offering 'nonperception' data, reflect less on the prevalence of corruption in a country and more on other factors, such as freedom of the press or the efficiency of the judicial system."

And that's the irony of the declining U.S. ranking.

Alleged corruption comes to light more in the United States, but the country still has a better record tackling bribery, both at home and abroad, than countries like Germany (15th) that rank higher.

"Bribes are paid by countries all over the world to do business," Boswell said. "U.S. enforcement is far more vigorous than anywhere else in the world."

Perceptions of corruption here rely on "our own sense of ourselves, and I think we have a pretty high standard," she added. "It's a wake-up call to the public and private sector that we need to make ethics and integrity more of a core value in the way we do business and remember that just because it's legal doesn't make it the right thing to do."

The top 25 least-corrupt countries in Transparency International's Corruption Perceptions Index 2010:

1. Denmark

1. New Zealand

1. Singapore

4. Finland

4. Sweden

6. Canada

7. Netherlands

8. Australia

10. Norway

11. Iceland

11. Luxembourg

13. Hong Kong

14. Ireland

15. Austria

15. Germany

17. Barbados

17. Japan

19. Qatar

20. United Kingdom

21. Chile

22. Belgium

22. United States

24. Uruguay

25. France

The bottom 25:

154. Cambodia

154. Central African Republic

154. Comoros

154. Congo-Brazzaville

154. Guinea-Bissau

154. Kenya

154. Laos

154. Papua New Guinea

154. Russia

154. Tajikistan

164. Democratic Republic of the Congo

164. Guinea

164. Kyrgyzstan

164. Venezuela

168. Angola

168. Equatorial Guinea

170. Burundi

171. Chad

172. Sudan

172. Turkmenistan

172. Uzbekistan

175. Iraq

176. Afghanistan

176. Myanmar

178. Somalia

Corporations Are Still Prohibited from Making Direct Contributions to Political Campaigns

Warren Richey and Linda Feldmann

Warren Richey and Linda Feldmann are staff writers for the Christian Science Monitor, *an international news organization.*

On Jan. 21 [2010], the US Supreme Court announced a landmark decision establishing for the first time that corporations enjoy the same First Amendment free-speech rights as individuals.

The 5-to-4 ruling in *Citizens United v. Federal Election Commission* has touched off dire predictions by campaign finance-reform advocates that campaigns for Congress and the presidency will soon be flooded with corporate dollars and influence.

Supporters of the decision say that the reformers' rhetoric is overblown and that the opinion reflects proper respect for free-speech principles.

Why Are Advocates of Campaign Finance Reform So Upset?

For nearly 40 years there has been a fundamental debate raging over how best to finance American political campaigns.

On one side, liberal reformers have sought to limit the influence of wealthy corporate interests by emphasizing the importance of maintaining a "level playing field." They have argued that corporations and labor unions could dominate the airwaves with slick and highly effective attack ads, leaving no time for the targeted candidates to respond. If American democracy is based on the principle of one person, one vote, they say, then corporations must be muzzled during political campaigns to prevent their amassed wealth from dominating and corrupting a political campaign.

Conservatives and libertarians, on the other hand, have countered that limiting the amount of money a corporation—or anyone—can spend to make their political point is censorship and a violation of the letter and spirit of the First Amendment's guarantee of free speech. Corporate power and influence aren't inherently corrupting, they say, as long as they're part of a vibrant debate within an open marketplace of ideas.

The debate most recently arose at the Supreme Court after the conservative advocacy group Citizens United, a corporation, was prevented from airing a 90-minute documentary critical of then candidate Hillary Rodham Clinton. The group wanted to air the film on pay-per-view cable television. The Federal Election Commission (FEC) determined that the documentary, *Hillary: The Movie*, was a form of electioneering that could be regulated under federal election laws. The FEC also ruled that advertisements about the film could be regulated, too. A panel of three federal judges upheld the FEC ruling. Citizens United then appealed to the Supreme Court.

Corporations and unions are still prohibited from making direct contributions to federal candidates.

High court decisions in 1990 and 2003 had strengthened the hand of those arguing for restrictions on corporations and for creation of a level campaign playing field. But other decisions since the 1970s advanced the idea that spending money in elections—even corporate money—can involve an expression of free speech.

What happened on Jan. 21 with the decision in *Citizens United v. FEC* is that five of the nine justices decided to erase the two key precedents that had laid the groundwork for reform focused on creating a level playing field. Those arguments have now been declared unconstitutional.

That's why campaign advocates of finance reform view the decision as akin to being pushed off a cliff. The decision marks the end of what had been a spirited debate over how to achieve the highest promise of American democracy.

Instead of a tightly regulated level playing field, the conservative wing of the Supreme Court has pointed America toward a messy "marketplace of ideas." In Justice Anthony Kennedy's view, if corporate speech presents a threat of undue influence in American politics, the proper response in the spirit of the First Amendment is to meet it with even more speech.

Won't Corporations Control Everything?

The Supreme Court did not jettison all campaign finance restrictions. Corporations and unions are still prohibited from making direct contributions to federal candidates. Such contributions must be made either by individuals or through regulated political action committees.

In addition, although corporations may now spend money to make a political point during election season, the high court has strongly endorsed—by an 8-to-1 vote—disclaimer and disclosure requirements within the federal campaign finance law.

That means that when corporations place a political ad on television or radio within 30 days of a primary or 60 days of a general election, it must include the disclaimer: "_____ is responsible for the content of this advertising."

This disclaimer requirement may deter many corporations from engaging in the kind of vicious political attack ads that some analysts suggest will now become commonplace.

But it may not deter those corporations organized to push an ideological agenda. In that case, such disclaimers will help ordinary voters assess the value of a particular message.

The high court also upheld a more sweeping disclosure requirement. Any corporation spending more than $10,000 a year on electioneering efforts must publicly disclose the names of individual contributors.

The disclaimer and disclosure laws were designed by Congress to help voters, the media, and others hold corporations—and their contributors—responsible for the content of their speech.

How Will the Ruling Affect Campaigns?

Corporations and unions will be able to spend directly, whenever they want, on advertising for and against presidential and congressional candidates. Laws governing corporate involvement in state campaigns will also presumably be struck down or repealed in the 24 states that have such laws. (Twenty-six states currently do not regulate corporate spending in their elections.)

Some analysts predict that, starting with this fall's campaigns, millions more corporate dollars will flood the media, benefiting Republicans more than Democrats. The money is likely to be funneled through trade associations and nonprofit groups, rather than deployed directly by the corporations, which will want to avoid closely associating their brands with a partisan position.

Opponents of the decision argue that, aside from the new influx of corporate money into campaigns, lobbyists will now be able to hold the threat of corporate-funded attack advertising over an elected official's head.

Other observers see less radical change ahead. Corporations have already effectively been influencing federal elections by funding issue ads, though in a more restricted manner.

Now, restrictions governing timing and content are gone, although disclosure rules remain.

The Supreme Court "took what had been a revolving door and took the door away altogether," says Evan Tracey, who tracks political advertising at the Campaign Media Analysis Group in Arlington, Va. "There was something there that slowed the money down. Now it's gone."

Who Benefits, and Who Loses?

Republicans, who tend to be friendlier to the interests of corporations, are the likely beneficiaries of this extra campaign spending. Democrats would benefit more than Republicans from greater union spending, although unions are not nearly as wealthy as major corporations.

Underfunded candidates who prove viable toward the end of a campaign may be helped with supportive advertising from outside groups, since the rule banning such ads less than 30 days before a primary and 60 days before a general election was struck down. This means there will probably be more competitive races.

Another big winner is the TV and radio industry. Mr. Tracey predicts as much as 20 percent more campaign ad spending in 2010 because of the ruling, or about $500 million—more than half of it to local outlets.

Can the Decision Be Overturned?

The current Supreme Court has spoken. But if one of the five justices in the majority on the decision were to leave and be replaced by a more liberal justice, the court could take a new campaign finance case and decide that corporations do not enjoy the free-speech rights of individuals.

Can Congress Affect the Impact of the Ruling?

Efforts are already under way to boost the power of small donors to counter the anticipated rise of corporate influence in elections. One bill, the Fair Elections Now Act, would create a voluntary public financing system for congressional elections. Candidates would qualify for federal matching funds by raising a large number of small donations in their communities.

Sen. Charles Schumer (D) of New York and Rep. Chris Van Hollen (D) of Maryland are planning to introduce legislation soon that would limit spending by contractors and corporations that received federal bailouts.

Other ideas include mandating shareholder approval for political spending and requiring CEOs [chief executive officers] and union leaders to appear in ads that they helped fund.

Money Did Not Buy Votes in the 2010 Midterm Congressional Elections

Robert Frank

Robert Frank is a senior writer for the Wall Street Journal *and is the author of* Richistan: A Journey Through the American Wealth Boom and the Lives of the New Rich.

"Never in the history of midterm elections have two candidates spent so much for so little."

That is how CBS News summed up the costly campaigns and ensuing defeats of California's Meg Whitman and Connecticut's Linda McMahon [in the 2010 midterm and state election].

Ms. Whitman, the former eBay chief, spent $142 million of her own money in a race for California governor. She lost to Jerry Brown, who mainly ran on his history and populism.

Ms. McMahon spent more than $41.5 million to run for the Senate but was defeated by the state's attorney general, Richard Blumenthal.

Carly Fiorina, the former H-P [Hewlett-Packard] chief who spent more than $1 million on her Senate campaign, failed to defeat the incumbent (and bigger spender) Barbara Boxer.

It wasn't all bad news for rich candidates. Florida's Rick Scott, the former health care chief who spent $73 million of his own cash, appears to have nudged past his Democratic opponent to become Florida's governor.

Money Cannot Buy Votes

Despite all the talk during the campaigns that the rich were buying political office, we have learned once again that money

Robert Frank, "Why Rich Candidates Failed," *Wall Street Journal*, November 3, 2010. Reproduced by permission of Dow Jones & Company, Inc.

can't buy votes. In this election season, with high unemployment and populist anger, personal wealth may have even been a detriment. Ms. Whitman had to deal with "maid-gate," the controversy surrounding her hiring and firing of an illegal-immigrant housecleaner. Ms. McMahon had to explain her unfortunately named family yacht [*Sexy Bitch*] and tough tactics as a professional wrestling tycoon.

Voters might have paid less attention to these issues during good times. But in today's economy, large wealth and the perception of being "out of touch" with the plight of the average American is a liability.

As one California voter . . . put it: "Meg came across as someone so different and out of touch with most Californians who are struggling to make ends meet yet still are interested enough in the future of the state to vote."

Why do you think wealthy candidates fared so badly in this midterm election?

CHAPTER 2

Is Corruption Destroying the US Financial System?

Chapter Preface

Beginning in 2007 the United States began sliding into an economic downturn considered by economists to be the worst financial crisis since the Great Depression of the 1930s. The Great Recession, as the crisis has been called, began when US housing prices, which had been rising dramatically for years, suddenly collapsed. This, in turn, caused securities related to real estate to plummet. These real estate securities were held by major banks, investment companies, and other financial institutions around the world; therefore, the housing collapse meant that many financial companies suffered huge losses, and some became completely insolvent. By the fall of 2008, for example, prominent US financial institutions including financial services firm Lehman Brothers, giant government-sponsored mortgage lending companies Fannie Mae and Freddie Mac, and insurer American International Group Inc. (AIG) had either filed for bankruptcy or barely survived. The financial crisis also led to significant decline in economic activity, marked by a stock market drop, a drying up of credit for businesses and individuals, and high unemployment. The US economic and financial problems quickly spread to the rest of the world, causing a global financial meltdown.

The US government responded aggressively to the crisis by bailing out some of the largest companies, passing fiscal stimulus programs, and expanding the money supply. In 2007, for example, the US Federal Reserve, the nation's central bank in charge of regulating the money supply, repeatedly cut its short-term interest rate, and the George W. Bush administration worked with Congress to pass an economic stimulus plan that sent out income tax rebate checks ($1200 for couples, plus $300 per child). In 2008 the federal government authorized $700 billion for the Troubled Asset Relief Program (TARP)—a massive program to rescue failing banks. Another federal program, known as the Term Asset-Backed Securities Loan Facility (TALF), authorized the Federal Reserve to purchase mortgage-backed securities and other assets held by financial institutions such as credit card or auto loan companies in order to stimulate the credit market. In 2009, while continuing to employ TARP and TALF monies, the incoming Barack Obama administration proposed and enacted another economic stimulus bill, the American Recovery and Reinvestment Act—a $787 billion package designed to boost economic growth with a mixture of tax cuts, aid to states, and infrastructure spending. In addition, the Federal Reserve directly bought up US debt to lower interest rates. According to the National Bureau of Economic Research, a nonpartisan economic research group that acts as the nation's economic analyst, the Great Recession ended in June 2009. However, as of late 2010, the US unemployment rate still hovered close to 10 percent and US economic growth was a modest 2.5 percent.

Critics argue that the true cause of the financial crisis was easy credit policies and a lack of regulatory oversight by the federal government. For example, many commentators criticize the Federal Reserve for keeping interest rates extremely low for many years—a policy that created the easy credit that allowed almost anyone to buy a home. In addition, many banks and mortgage originators encouraged home buyers to apply for high-risk, subprime loans, quickly selling them to other financial institutions such as Wall Street investment banks and other large investment companies. These investment companies bundled the loans together and advertised them as high-quality, low-risk, mortgage-backed securities that they in turn sold for large profits around the world. Critics charge that the government failed to regulate these high-risk mortgage securities and that neither Congress nor the Securities and Exchange Commission—the federal agency charged with regulating securities—exercised proper oversight over this investment scheme. Many critics attribute this lax regulation to a type of legal corruption—millions of dollars spent by financial corporations on lobbying, political advertising, and campaign contributions for the purpose of buying influence with the US Congress and federal regulators.

The US financial crisis and Wall Street's influence over the US government have now become hotly debated topics among experts, policy makers, and the public. The authors of the viewpoints in this chapter discuss whether corruption is destroying the US financial sector.

There Is Rampant Corruption on Wall Street

Michael Snyder

Michael Snyder is editor of The Economic Collapse, *a blog that provides commentary on the US and world economies.*

If you ask most Americans, they will agree that the financial system is corrupt. It is generally assumed that just like most politicians, most big bankers are corrupt by nature.

But the truth is that the vast majority of Americans have no idea just how corrupt the U.S. financial system has become.

The reality is that the American Dream is literally being stolen from millions of Americans right out from under their noses and they don't even realize it. The corruption on Wall Street has become so deep and so vast that it is hard to even find the words to describe it. The level of greed being displayed by many Wall Street firms would make Gordon Gecko [a fictional character in the movie *Wall Street*] blush. It seems that the major financial players will try just about anything these days—as long as they think they can get away with it. But in the process they are contributing to the destruction of the greatest economic machine that the planet has ever seen.

Eleven Examples of the Insane Corruption on Wall Street

1. *Price manipulation of gold and silver.* An industry insider "whistle-blower" has come forward with "smoking-gun" evidence that major financial institutions have been openly and blatantly manipulating the price of gold and silver. But so far

Michael Snyder, "11 Examples of How Insanely Corrupt the U.S. Financial System Has Become," *Business Insider*, April 14, 2010. Reproduced by permission.

those who are supposed to be regulating these firms have been sitting back and doing nothing about it.

2. *"Gold deposits" with no relation to actual gold.* It has also now come out that most "gold" that is traded on the markets is not backed by the actual metal itself. For years, most people have assumed that the London Bullion Market Association [LBMA], the world's largest gold market, had actual gold to back up the massive "gold deposits" at the major LBMA banks. But that is not the truth at all. Industry insiders are now revealing that LBMA banks actually have approximately a hundred times more gold deposits than actual gold bullion. When most people think they are buying gold what they are actually buying is pieces of paper that say that they own gold. Meanwhile they are being charged huge storage fees to store the gold.

The corruption at Goldman Sachs is very deep and very entrenched, but they will never be fully investigated because they have such close ties to the U.S. government.

---

3. *No punishment for AIG-destroyer Joe Cassano.* The guy who helped bring down AIG [a large US insurance company] is going to get off scot-free and will be able to keep the millions in profits that he made in the process. It must be nice to be him.

4. *Backstab hedging at Goldman Sachs.* Goldman Sachs [a global investment firm based in the United States] is denying that it "bet against its clients" when it changed its position in the housing market in 2007. But the reality is that is exactly when they did and a lot of things that are even worse than that. The corruption at Goldman Sachs is very deep and very entrenched, but they will never be fully investigated because they have such close ties to the U.S. government.

5. *Predatory deals against American cities.* It is being alleged that the biggest banks in the United States are ripping off

American cities with the same predatory deals that brought down the financial system of Greece. Of course the big banks will rip off just about anyone these days if they think they can get away with it.

6. *"Repo 105."* Several major Wall Street banks are being accused of using accounting techniques similar to those utilized by Lehman Brothers [a global financial services firm that filed for bankruptcy during the recent financial crisis] in its final days to mask the size of their balance sheets at the end of reporting periods.

7. *The Federal Reserve Ponzi scheme.* The Federal Reserve [America's central bank in charge of the U.S. money supply] bought up the vast majority of U.S. government debt in 2009. Many analysts claim that this is the same as "printing money out of thin air," while others are openly calling it a Ponzi scheme [fraudulent investments where investors are not paid from actual profits].

8. *Even the Fed bets on state defaults.* It turns out that the Federal Reserve holds credit default swaps on the debt of Florida schools, and on debt owed by the states of California and Nevada. So the Federal Reserve would profit if one of those states defaulted on its debt. Talk about a conflict of interest.

9. *Record bonuses during and after the financial crisis.* Executives at many of the firms that received large amounts of money during the Wall Street bailouts are being lavished with record bonuses as millions of other average Americans are suffering intensely. Even the CEOs [chief executive officers] of bailed-out regional banks are getting big raises.

10. *Invasive data mining by credit card companies.* We may not know much about what is going on inside some of these banks, but they sure do know a lot about us. For example, it has been revealed that the data mining operations of the major credit card companies are becoming so sophisticated that they can actually predict how likely you are to get a divorce.

11. *A national debt that dooms our children.* But the biggest financial fraud of all is being committed against the American people. The exploding U.S. national debt threatens to destroy the financial future of literally generations of Americans. It is obscenely immoral to saddle our children and our grandchildren with the biggest mountain of debt in the history of the world. If they get the chance, future generations of Americans will look back and curse this generation for what we have done to them.

Financial Deregulation by a Corrupt Congress and the Executive Branch Led to the US Financial Meltdown

Essential Information and the Consumer Education Foundation

Essential Information is a nonprofit organization that promotes a just economy. The Consumer Education Foundation is a nonprofit consumer research, education, and advocacy organization.

Blame Wall Street for the current financial crisis. Investment banks, hedge funds and commercial banks made reckless bets using borrowed money. They created and trafficked in exotic investment vehicles that even top Wall Street executives—not to mention firm directors—did not understand. They hid risky investments in off-balance-sheet vehicles or capitalized on their legal status to cloak investments altogether. They engaged in unconscionable predatory lending that offered huge profits for a time, but led to dire consequences when the loans proved unpayable. And they created, maintained and justified a housing bubble, the bursting of which has thrown the United States and the world into a deep recession, resulted in a foreclosure epidemic ripping apart communities across the country.

Financial Deregulation at Fault

But while Wall Street is culpable for the financial crisis and global recession, others do share responsibility.

For the last three decades, financial regulators, Congress and the executive branch have steadily eroded the regulatory

Essential Information and the Consumer Education Foundation, "Sold Out: How Wall Street and Washington Betrayed America," March 4, 2009. www.essential.org. Reproduced by permission.

system that restrained the financial sector from acting on its own worst tendencies. The post-Depression regulatory system aimed to force disclosure of publicly relevant financial information; established limits on the use of leverage; drew bright lines between different kinds of financial activity and protected regulated commercial banking from investment bank-style risk taking; enforced meaningful limits on economic concentration, especially in the banking sector; provided meaningful consumer protections (including restrictions on usurious interest rates); and contained the financial sector so that it remained subordinate to the real economy. This hodge-podge regulatory system was, of course, highly imperfect, including because it too often failed to deliver on its promises.

The financial sector showered campaign contributions on politicians from both parties, invested heavily in a legion of lobbyists, [and] paid academics and think tanks to justify their preferred policy positions.

But it was not its imperfections that led to the erosion and collapse of that regulatory system. It was a concerted effort by Wall Street, steadily gaining momentum until it reached fever pitch in the late 1990s and continued right through the first half of 2008. Even now, Wall Street continues to defend many of its worst practices. Though it bows to the political reality that new regulation is coming, it aims to reduce the scope and importance of that regulation and, if possible, use the guise of regulation to further remove public controls over its operations.

This [viewpoint] has one overriding message: financial deregulation led directly to the financial meltdown. . . .

Wall Street's Political Muscle

The details matter. The report documents a dozen specific deregulatory steps (including failures to regulate and failures to enforce existing regulations) that enabled Wall Street to crash the financial system. Second, Wall Street didn't obtain these regulatory abeyances based on the force of its arguments. At every step, critics warned of the dangers of further deregulation. Their evidence-based claims could not offset the political and economic muscle of Wall Street. The financial sector showered campaign contributions on politicians from both parties, invested heavily in a legion of lobbyists, paid academics and think tanks to justify their preferred policy positions, and cultivated a pliant media—especially a cheerleading business media complex. . . .

Campaign Contributions and Lobbying

The aggregate data are startling: The financial sector invested more than $5.1 billion in political influence purchasing over the last decade.

The entire financial sector (finance, insurance, real estate) drowned political candidates in campaign contributions over the past decade, spending more than $1.7 billion in federal elections from 1998–2008. Primarily reflecting the balance of power over the decade, about 55 percent went to Republicans and 45 percent to Democrats. Democrats took just more than half of the financial sector's 2008 election cycle contributions.

The financial sector employed 2,996 lobbyists in 2007 . . . [many of them] former government officials.

The industry spent even more—topping $3.4 billion—on officially registered lobbying of federal officials during the same period.

During the period 1998–2008:

- Accounting firms spent $81 million on campaign contributions and $122 million on lobbying;

- Commercial banks spent more than $155 million on campaign contributions, while investing nearly $383 million in officially registered lobbying;

- Insurance companies donated more than $220 million and spent more than $1.1 billion on lobbying;

- Securities firms invested nearly $513 million in campaign contributions, and an additional $600 million in lobbying.

All this money went to hire legions of lobbyists. The financial sector employed 2,996 lobbyists in 2007. Financial firms employed an extraordinary number of former government officials as lobbyists. This report finds 142 of the lobbyists employed by the financial sector from 1998–2008 were previously high-ranking officials or employees in the executive branch or Congress.

Twelve Deregulatory Steps to Financial Meltdown

1. *Repeal of the Glass-Steagall Act and the Rise of the Culture of Recklessness*

The Financial Services Modernization Act of 1999 [also known as the Gramm-Leach-Bliley Act] formally repealed the Glass-Steagall Act of 1933 (also known as the Banking Act of 1933) and related laws, which prohibited commercial banks from offering investment banking and insurance services. In a form of corporate civil disobedience, Citibank and insurance giant Travelers Group merged in 1998—a move that was illegal at the time, but for which they were given a two-year forbearance—on the assumption that they would be able to force a change in the relevant law at a future date. They did. The 1999 repeal of Glass-Steagall helped create the conditions in which banks invested monies from checking and savings accounts into creative financial instruments such as mortgage-backed securities and credit default swaps, investment gambles that rocked the financial markets in 2008.

2. *Hiding Liabilities: Off-Balance-Sheet Accounting*

Holding assets off the balance sheet generally allows companies to exclude "toxic" or money-losing assets from financial disclosures to investors in order to make the company appear more valuable than it is. Banks used off-balance-sheet operations—special purpose entities (SPEs), or special purpose vehicles (SPVs)—to hold securitized mortgages. Because the securitized mortgages were held by an off-balance-sheet entity, however, the banks did not have to hold capital reserves as against the risk of default—thus leaving them so vulnerable. Off-balance-sheet operations are permitted by Financial Accounting Standards Board rules installed at the urging of big banks. The Securities Industry and Financial Markets Association and the American Securitization Forum are among the lobby interests now blocking efforts to get this rule reformed.

3. *The Executive Branch Rejects Financial Derivative Regulation*

Financial derivatives are unregulated. By all accounts this has been a disaster, as [prominent investor] Warren Buffett's warning that they represent "weapons of mass financial destruction" has proven prescient. Financial derivatives have amplified the financial crisis far beyond the unavoidable troubles connected to the popping of the housing bubble.

The Commodity Futures Trading Commission (CFTC) has jurisdiction over futures, options and other derivatives connected to commodities. During the [Bill] Clinton administration, the CFTC sought to exert regulatory control over financial derivatives. The agency was quashed by opposition from Treasury Secretary Robert Rubin and, above all, Fed [Federal Reserve] Chair Alan Greenspan. They challenged the agency's jurisdictional authority and insisted that CFTC regulation might imperil existing financial activity that was already at considerable scale (though nowhere near present levels). Then

Deputy Treasury Secretary Lawrence Summers told Congress that CFTC proposals "cas[t] a shadow of regulatory uncertainty over an otherwise thriving market."

4. *Congress Blocks Financial Derivative Regulation*

The deregulation—or nonregulation—of financial derivatives was sealed in 2000, with the Commodities Futures Modernization Act (CFMA), passage of which was engineered by then Senator Phil Gramm, R-Texas. The Commodities Futures Modernization Act exempts financial derivatives, including credit default swaps, from regulation and helped create the current financial crisis.

5. *The SEC's Voluntary Regulation Regime for Investment Banks*

In 1975, the SEC's [Securities and Exchange Commission's] trading and markets division promulgated a rule requiring investment banks to maintain a debt-to-net-capital ratio of less than 12 to 1. It forbid trading in securities if the ratio reached or exceeded 12 to 1, so most companies maintained a ratio far below it. In 2004, however, the SEC succumbed to a push from the big investment banks—led by [investment firm] Goldman Sachs, and its then chair, Henry Paulson—and authorized investment banks to develop their own net capital requirements in accordance with standards published by the Basel Committee on Banking Supervision. This essentially involved complicated mathematical formulas that imposed no real limits, and was voluntarily administered. With this new freedom, investment banks pushed borrowing ratios to as high as 40 to 1, as in the case of [investment company] Merrill Lynch. This superleverage not only made the investment banks more vulnerable when the housing bubble popped, it enabled the banks to create a more tangled mess of derivative investments—so that their individual failures, or the potential of failure, became systemic crises. Former SEC Chair Chris Cox has acknowledged that the voluntary regulation was a complete failure.

6. *Bank Self-Regulation Goes Global: Preparing to Repeat the Meltdown?*

In 1988, global bank regulators adopted a set of rules known as Basel I, to impose a minimum global standard of capital adequacy for banks. Complicated financial maneuvering made it hard to determine compliance, however, which led to negotiations over a new set of regulations. Basel II, heavily influenced by the banks themselves, establishes varying capital reserve requirements, based on subjective factors of agency ratings and the banks' own internal risk-assessment models. The SEC experience with Basel II principles illustrates their fatal flaws. Commercial banks in the United States are supposed to be compliant with aspects of Basel II as of April 2008, but complications and intra-industry disputes have slowed implementation.

7. *Failure to Prevent Predatory Lending*

Even in a deregulated environment, the banking regulators retained authority to crack down on predatory lending abuses. Such enforcement activity would have protected homeowners, and lessened though not prevented the current financial crisis. But the regulators sat on their hands. The Federal Reserve took three formal actions against subprime lenders from 2002 to 2007. The Office of the Comptroller of the Currency [OCC], which has authority over almost 1,800 banks, took three consumer-protection enforcement actions from 2004 to 2006.

8. *Federal Preemption of State Consumer Protection Laws*

When the states sought to fill the vacuum created by federal nonenforcement of consumer protection laws against predatory lenders, the feds jumped to stop them. "In 2003," as Eliot Spitzer [a political commentator] recounted, "during the height of the predatory lending crisis, the Office of the Comptroller of the Currency invoked a clause from the 1863 National Banking Act to issue formal opinions preempting all state predatory lending laws, thereby rendering them inoperative. The OCC also promulgated new rules that prevented states from enforcing any of their own consumer protection laws against national banks."

9. *Escaping Accountability: Assignee Liability*

Under existing federal law, with only limited exceptions, only the original mortgage lender is liable for any predatory and illegal features of a mortgage—even if the mortgage is transferred to another party. This arrangement effectively immunized acquirers of the mortgage ("assignees") for any problems with the initial loan, and relieved them of any duty to investigate the terms of the loan. Wall Street interests could purchase, bundle and securitize subprime loans—including many with pernicious, predatory terms—without fear of liability for illegal loan terms. The arrangement left victimized borrowers with no cause of action against any but the original lender, and typically with no defenses against being foreclosed upon. Representative Bob Ney, R-Ohio—a close friend of Wall Street who subsequently went to prison in connection with the [Jack] Abramoff scandal—was the leading opponent of a fair assignee liability regime.

10. *Fannie and Freddie Enter the Subprime Market*

At the peak of the housing boom, [government-sponsored corporations] Fannie Mae [Federal National Mortgage Association] and Freddie Mac [Federal Home Loan Mortgage Corporation] were dominant purchasers in the subprime secondary market. The government-sponsored enterprises were followers, not leaders, but they did end up taking on substantial subprime assets—at least $57 billion. The purchase of subprime assets was a break from prior practice, justified by theories of expanded access to homeownership for low-income families and rationalized by mathematical models allegedly able to identify and assess risk to newer levels of precision. In fact, the motivation was the for-profit nature of the institutions and their particular executive incentive schemes. Massive lobbying—including especially but not only of Democratic friends of the institutions—enabled them to divert from their traditional exclusive focus on prime loans.

Fannie and Freddie are not responsible for the financial crisis. They are responsible for their own demise, and the resultant massive taxpayer liability.

11. *Merger Mania*

The effective abandonment of antitrust and related regulatory principles over the last two decades has enabled a remarkable concentration in the banking sector, even in advance of recent moves to combine firms as a means to preserve the functioning of the financial system. The megabanks achieved too-big-to-fail status. While this should have meant they be treated as public utilities requiring heightened regulation and risk control, other deregulatory maneuvers (including repeal of Glass-Steagall) enabled these gigantic institutions to benefit from explicit and implicit federal guarantees, even as they pursued reckless high-risk investments.

12. *Rampant Conflicts of Interest: Credit Ratings Firms' Failure*

Credit ratings are a key link in the financial crisis story. With Wall Street combining mortgage loans into pools of securitized assets and then slicing them up into tranches, the resultant financial instruments were attractive to many buyers because they promised high returns. But pension funds and other investors could only enter the game if the securities were highly rated.

The credit rating firms enabled these investors to enter the game, by attaching high ratings to securities that actually were high risk—as subsequent events have revealed. The credit ratings firms have a bias to offering favorable ratings to new instruments because of their complex relationships with issuers, and their desire to maintain and obtain other business dealings with issuers.

This institutional failure and conflict of interest might and should have been forestalled by the SEC, but the Credit Rating

Agency Reform Act of 2006 gave the SEC insufficient oversight authority. In fact, the SEC must give an approval rating to credit ratings agencies if they are adhering to their own standards—even if the SEC knows those standards to be flawed.

Controlling Wall Street

Wall Street is presently humbled, but not prostrate. Despite siphoning trillions of dollars from the public purse, Wall Street executives continue to warn about the perils of restricting "financial innovation"—even though it was these very innovations that led to the crisis. And they are scheming to use the coming congressional focus on financial regulation to centralize authority with industry-friendly agencies.

If we are to see the meaningful regulation we need, Congress must adopt the view that Wall Street has no legitimate seat at the table. With Wall Street having destroyed the system that enriched its high flyers, and plunged the global economy into deep recession, it's time for Congress to tell Wall Street that its political investments have also gone bad. This time, legislating must be to control Wall Street, not further Wall Street's control.

President Barack Obama Is Continuing to Empower Corrupt Wall Street Insiders

Glenn Greenwald

Glenn Greenwald is a US lawyer, an author, and a columnist and blogger at Salon.com, where he focuses on political and legal topics.

White House officials yesterday [April 3, 2010] released their personal financial disclosure forms, and included in the millions of dollars which top [President Barack] Obama economics adviser Larry Summers made from Wall Street in 2008 is this detail:

> Lawrence H. Summers, one of President Obama's top economic advisers, collected roughly $5.2 million in compensation from hedge fund D.E. Shaw over the past year and was paid more than $2.7 million in speaking fees by several troubled Wall Street firms and other organizations. . . .

> Financial institutions including JPMorgan Chase, Citigroup, Goldman Sachs, Lehman Brothers and Merrill Lynch paid Summers for speaking appearances in 2008. Fees ranged from $45,000 for a Nov. 12 Merrill Lynch appearance to $135,000 for an April 16 visit to Goldman Sachs, according to his disclosure form.

That's $135,000 paid by [investment firm] Goldman Sachs to Summers—for a one-day visit. And the payment was made at a time—in April 2008—when everyone assumed that the next president would either be Barack Obama or Hillary Clinton and that Larry Summers would therefore become exactly

Glenn Greenwald, "Larry Summers, Tim Geithner, and Wall Street's Ownership of Government," *Salon.com*, April 4, 2010. This article first appeared in Salon.com, at http://www.Salon.com. An online version remains in the Salon archives. Reprinted with permission.

what he now is: the most influential financial official in the U.S. government (and the $45,000 Merrill Lynch payment came 8 days *after Obama's election*). Goldman would not be able to make a one-day $135,000 payment to Summers now that he is Obama's top economic adviser, but doing so a few months beforehand was obviously something about which neither parties felt any compunction. It's basically an advanced bribe. And it's paying off in spades. And none of it seemed to bother Obama in the slightest when he first strongly considered naming Summers as Treasury Secretary and then named him his top economic adviser instead (thereby avoiding the need for Senate confirmation), knowing that Summers would exert great influence in determining who benefited from the government's response to the financial crisis.

[Financial] corruption is so tawdry and transparent . . . that it is mystifying that it is not provoking more mass public rage.

Fraud and Deregulation

Last night, former [Ronald] Reagan-era S&L [savings and loan] regulator and current University of Missouri Professor Bill Black was on *Bill Moyers' Journal* and detailed the magnitude of what he called the ongoing massive fraud, the role Tim Geithner played in it before being promoted to Treasury Secretary (where he continues to abet it), and—most amazingly of all—the crusade led by Alan Greenspan, former Goldman CEO Robert Rubin (Geithner's mentor) and Larry Summers in the late 1990s to block the efforts of top regulators (especially Brooksley Born, head of the Commodities Futures Trading Commission) to regulate the exact financial derivatives market that became the principal cause of the global financial crisis. To get a sense for how deep and massive is the ongoing fraud and the key role played in it by key Obama officials, I highly recommend watching that Black interview.

This article from *Stanford Magazine*—an absolutely amazing read—details how Summers, Rubin and Greenspan led the way in blocking any regulatory efforts of the derivatives market whatsoever on the ground that the financial industry and its lobbyists were objecting:

> As chairperson of the CFTC [Commodity Futures Trading Commission], Born advocated reining in the huge and growing market for financial derivatives. . . . One type of derivative—known as a credit default swap—has been a key contributor to the economy's recent unraveling. . . .
>
> Back in the 1990s, however, Born's proposal stirred an almost visceral response from other regulators in the [Bill] Clinton administration, as well as members of Congress and lobbyists. . . . But even the modest proposal got a vituperative response. The dozen or so large banks that wrote most of the OTC [over-the-counter] derivative contracts [a type of risky security] saw the move as a threat to a major profit center. Greenspan and his deregulation-minded brain trust saw no need to upset the status quo. The sheer act of contemplating regulation, they maintained, would cause widespread chaos in markets around the world.
>
> Born recalls taking a phone call from Lawrence Summers, then Rubin's top deputy at the Treasury Department, complaining about the proposal, and mentioning that he was taking heat from industry lobbyists. . . . The debate came to a head April 21, 1998. In a Treasury Department meeting of a presidential working group that included Born and the other top regulators, Greenspan and Rubin took turns attempting to change her mind. Rubin took the lead, she recalls.
>
> "I was told by the secretary of the treasury that the CFTC had no jurisdiction, and for that reason and that reason

alone, we should not go forward," Born says. . . . "It seemed totally inexplicable to me," Born says of the seeming disinterest her counterparts showed in how the markets were operating. "It was as though the other financial regulators were saying, 'We don't want to know.'"

She formally launched the proposal on May 7, and within hours, Greenspan, Rubin and [SEC chairman Arthur] Levitt issued a joint statement condemning Born and the CFTC, expressing "grave concern about this action and its possible consequences." They announced a plan to ask for legislation to stop the CFTC in its tracks.

Rubin, Summers and Greenspan succeeded in inducing Congress—funded, of course, by these same financial firms—to enact legislation blocking the CFTC from regulating these derivative markets. More amazingly still, the CFTC, headed back then by Born, is now headed by Obama appointee Gary Gensler, a former Goldman Sachs executive (naturally) who was as instrumental as anyone in blocking any regulations of those derivative markets (and then enriched himself by feeding on those unregulated markets).

Just think about how this works. People like Rubin, Summers and Gensler shuffle back and forth from the public to the private sector and back again, repeatedly switching places with their GOP [Republican] counterparts in this endless public/private sector looting. When in government, they ensure that the laws and regulations are written to redound directly to the benefit of a handful of Wall St. firms, literally abolishing all safeguards and allowing them to pillage and steal. Then, when out of government, they return to those very firms and collect millions upon millions of dollars, profits made possible by the laws and regulations they implemented when in government. Then, when their party returns to power, they return back to government, where they continue to use their influence to ensure that the oligarchical circle that rewards them so massively is protected and advanced. This corruption is so tawdry and transparent—and it has fueled and continues to fuel a fraud so enormous and destructive as to be unprecedented in both size and audacity—that it is mystifying that is not provoking more mass public rage.

[Secretary of the Treasury Timothy] Geithner . . . was one of our nation's top regulators, during the entire subprime scandal, . . . [but] he took absolutely no effective action.

The Obama Administration's Protection of Wrongdoers

All of that leads to things like this, from today's *Washington Post*:

The Obama administration is engineering its new bailout initiatives in a way that it believes will allow firms benefiting from the programs to avoid restrictions imposed by Congress, including limits on lavish executive pay, according to government officials. . . .

The administration believes it can sidestep the rules because, in many cases, it has decided not to provide federal aid directly to financial companies, the sources said. Instead, the government has set up special entities that act as middlemen, channeling the bailout funds to the firms and, via this two-step process, stripping away the requirement that the restrictions be imposed, according to officials. . . .

In one program, designed to restart small-business lending, President Obama's officials are planning to set up a middleman called a special purpose vehicle—a term made notorious during the Enron scandal—or another type of entity to evade the congressional mandates, sources familiar with the matter said.

If that isn't illegal, it is as close to it as one can get. And it is a blatant attempt by the White House to brush aside—circumvent and violate—the spirit if not the letter of congressional restrictions on executive pay for TARP [Troubled Asset Relief Program]-receiving firms. It was Obama, in the wake of various scandals over profligate spending by TARP firms, who pretended to ride the wave of populist anger and to lead the way in demanding limits on compensation. And ever since his flamboyant announcement, Obama—adopting the same approach that seems to drive him in most other areas—has taken one step after the next to gut and render irrelevant the very compensation limits he publicly pretended to champion (thereafter dishonestly blaming Chris Dodd for doing so and virtually destroying Dodd's political career). And the winners—as always—are the same Wall St. firms that caused the crisis in the first place while enriching and otherwise co-opting the very individuals Obama chose to be his top financial officials.

Obama railed against precisely this sort of incestuous, profoundly corrupt control by narrow private interests of the government, yet he has chosen to empower the very individuals who most embody that corruption.

Worse still, what is happening here is an exact analog to what is happening in the realm of [President George W.] Bush war crimes—the Obama administration's first priority is to protect the wrongdoers and criminals by ensuring that the criminality remains secret. Here is how Black explained it last night:

> [*Professor Bill*] *Black*: Geithner is charging, is covering up. Just like Paulson did before him. Geithner is publicly saying that it's going to take $2 trillion—a trillion is a thousand billion—$2 trillion taxpayer dollars to deal with this problem. But they're allowing all the banks to report that they're

not only solvent, but fully capitalized. Both statements can't be true. It can't be that they need $2 trillion, because they have mass losses, and that they're fine.

These are all people who have failed. Paulson failed, Geithner failed. They were all promoted because they failed, not because . . .

[TV host Bill] *Moyers*: What do you mean?

Black: Well, Geithner has, was one of our nation's top regulators, during the entire subprime scandal, that I just described. He took absolutely no effective action. He gave no warning. He did nothing in response to the FBI [Federal Bureau of Investigation] warning that there was an epidemic of fraud. All this pig in the poke stuff happened under him. So, in his phrase about legacy assets. Well he's a failed legacy regulator. . . .

The Great Depression, we said, "Hey, we have to learn the facts. What caused this disaster, so that we can take steps, like pass the Glass-Steagall law, that will prevent future disasters?" Where's our investigation?

What would happen if after a plane crash, we said, "Oh, we don't want to look in the past. We want to be forward looking. Many people might have been, you know, we don't want to pass blame. No. We have a nonpartisan, skilled inquiry. We spend lots of money on, get really bright people. And we find out, to the best of our ability, what caused every single major plane crash in America. And because of that, aviation has an extraordinarily good safety record. We ought to follow the same policies in the financial sphere. We have to find out what caused the disasters, or we will keep reliving them. . . .

Moyers: Yeah. Are you saying that Timothy Geithner, the Secretary of the Treasury, and others in the administration, with the banks, are engaged in a coverup to keep us from knowing what went wrong?

Black: Absolutely.

Moyers: You are.

Black: Absolutely, because they are scared to death. . . . What we're doing with—no, Treasury and both administrations. The Bush administration and now the Obama administration kept secret from us what was being done with AIG. AIG was being used secretly to bail out favored banks like UBS and like Goldman Sachs. Secretary Paulson's firm, that he had come from being CEO. It got the largest amount of money. $12.9 billion. And they didn't want us to know that. And it was only congressional pressure, and not congressional pressure, by the way, on Geithner, but congressional pressure on AIG.

Where Congress said, "We will not give you a single penny more unless we know who received the money." And, you know, when he was Treasury Secretary, Paulson created a recommendation group to tell Treasury what they ought to do with AIG. And he put Goldman Sachs on it.

Moyers: Even though Goldman Sachs had a big vested stake.

Black: Massive stake. And even though he had just been CEO of Goldman Sachs before becoming Treasury Secretary. Now, in most stages in American history, that would be a scandal of such proportions that he wouldn't be allowed in civilized society.

This is exactly what former IMF [International Monetary Fund] Chief Economist Simon Johnson warned about in his vital *Atlantic* article: "that the finance industry has effectively captured our government—a state of affairs that more typically describes emerging markets, and is at the center of many emerging-market crises." This is the key passage where Johnson described the hallmark of how corrupt oligarchies that cause financial crises then attempt to deal with the fallout:

Squeezing the oligarchs, though, is seldom the strategy of choice among emerging-market governments. Quite the contrary: at the outset of the crisis, *the oligarchs are usually among the first to get extra help from the government, such as preferential access to foreign currency, or maybe a nice tax break*, or—here's a classic Kremlin bailout technique—*the assumption of private debt obligations* by the government under duress, generosity toward old friends takes many innovative forms. Meanwhile, needing to squeeze someone, most emerging-market governments look first to ordinary working folk—at least until the riots grow too large. . . .

As much as he campaigned against anything, Obama railed against precisely this sort of incestuous, profoundly corrupt control by narrow private interests of the government, yet he has chosen to empower the very individuals who most embody that corruption. And the results are exactly what one would expect them to be.

Legislative Reforms Will Control Wall Street Excesses

Barack Obama

Barack Obama is the forty-fourth and current president of the United States.

We are gathered in the heart of our nation's capital, surrounded by memorials to leaders and citizens who served our nation in its earliest days and in its days of greatest trial. Today is such a time for America.

A Severe Recession

Over the past two years, we have faced the worst recession since the Great Depression. Eight million people lost their jobs. Tens of millions saw the value of their homes and retirement savings plummet. Countless businesses have been unable to get the loans they need and many have been forced to shut their doors. And although the economy is growing again, too many people are still feeling the pain of the downturn.

Now, while a number of factors led to such a severe recession, the primary cause was a breakdown in our financial system. It was a crisis born of a failure of responsibility from certain corners of Wall Street to the halls of power in Washington. For years, our financial sector was governed by antiquated and poorly enforced rules that allowed some to game the system and take risks that endangered the entire economy.

Unscrupulous lenders locked consumers into complex loans with hidden costs. [Financial] firms like AIG [American International Group Inc.] placed massive, risky bets with borrowed money. And while the rules left abuse and excess un-

Barack Obama, "Remarks by the President at Signing of Dodd-Frank Wall Street Reform and Consumer Protection Act, Ronald Reagan Building," *White House Press*, July 21, 2010. WhiteHouse.gov.

checked, they also left taxpayers on the hook if a big bank or financial institution ever failed.

Financial Reform

Now, even before the crisis hit, I went to Wall Street and I called for commonsense reforms to protect consumers and our economy as a whole. And soon after taking office, I proposed a set of reforms to empower consumers and investors, to bring the shadowy deals that caused this crisis into the light of day, and to put a stop to taxpayer bailouts once and for all. Today, thanks to a lot of people in this room, those reforms will become the law of the land.

For the last year, Chairmen Barney Frank and Chris Dodd have worked day and night . . . to bring about this reform. And I am profoundly grateful to them. I would be remiss if I didn't also express my appreciation to Senator Harry Reid and Speaker [of the House] Nancy Pelosi for their leadership. It wouldn't have happened without them.

Passing this bill was no easy task. To get there, we had to overcome the furious lobbying of an array of powerful interest groups and a partisan minority determined to block change. So the members who are here today, both on the stage and in the audience, they have done a great service in devoting so much time and expertise to this effort, to looking out for the public interests and not the special interests. And I also want to thank the three Republican senators who put partisanship aside, judged this bill on the merits, and voted for reform. We're grateful to them. And the Republican House members. . . .

Now, let's put this in perspective. The fact is, the financial industry is central to our nation's ability to grow, to prosper, to compete and to innovate. There are a lot of banks that understand and fulfill this vital role, and there are a whole lot of bankers who want to do right—and do right—by their customers. This reform will help foster innovation, not hamper it. It is designed to make sure that everybody follows the same set of rules, so that firms compete on price and quality, not on tricks and not on traps.

It demands accountability and responsibility from everyone. It provides certainty to everybody, from bankers to farmers to business owners to consumers. And unless your business model depends on cutting corners or bilking your customers, you've got nothing to fear from reform.

Help for Consumers, Curbing Financial Abuse, and Transparency

Now, for all those Americans who are wondering what Wall Street reform means for you, here's what you can expect. If you've ever applied for a credit card, a student loan, or a mortgage, you know the feeling of signing your name to pages of barely understandable fine print. What often happens as a result is that many Americans are caught by hidden fees and penalties, or saddled with loans they can't afford.

That's what happened to Robin Fox, hit with a massive rate increase on her credit card balance even though she paid her bills on time. That's what happened to Andrew Giordano, who discovered hundreds of dollars in overdraft fees on his bank statement—fees he had no idea he might face. Both are here today. Well, with this law, unfair rate hikes, like the one that hit Robin, will end for good. And we'll ensure that people like Andrew aren't unwittingly caught by overdraft fees when they sign up for a checking account.

With this law, we'll crack down on abusive practices in the mortgage industry. We'll make sure that contracts are simpler—putting an end to many hidden penalties and fees in complex mortgages—so folks know what they're signing.

With this law, students who take out college loans will be provided clear and concise information about their obligations.

And with this law, ordinary investors—like seniors and folks saving for retirement—will be able to receive more information about the costs and risks of mutual funds and other investment products, so that they can make better financial decisions as to what will work for them.

Reform will ... rein in the abuse and excess that nearly brought down our financial system.

So, all told, those reforms represent the strongest consumer financial protections in history. In history. And these protections will be enforced by a new consumer watchdog with just one job: looking out for people—not big banks, not lenders, not investment houses—looking out for people as they interact with the financial system.

And that's not just good for consumers: that's good for the economy. Because reform will put a stop to a lot of the bad loans that fueled a debt-based bubble. And it will mean all companies will have to seek customers by offering better products, instead of more deceptive ones.

Now, beyond the consumer protections I've outlined, reform will also rein in the abuse and excess that nearly brought down our financial system. It will finally bring transparency to the kinds of complex and risky transactions that helped trigger the financial crisis. Shareholders will also have a greater say on the pay of CEOs [chief executive officers] and other executives, so they can reward success, instead of failure.

And finally, because of this law, the American people will never again be asked to foot the bill for Wall Street's mistakes. There will be no more tax-funded bailouts—period. If a large financial institution should ever fail, this reform gives us the ability to wind it down without endangering the broader economy. And there will be new rules to make clear that no firm is somehow protected because it is "too big to fail," so we don't have another AIG.

Clear Rules and Basic Safeguards

That's what this reform will mean. Now, it doesn't mean our work is over. For these new rules to be effective, regulators will have to be vigilant. We may need to make adjustments along the way as our financial system adapts to these new changes and changes around the globe. No law can force anybody to be responsible: it's still incumbent on those on Wall Street to heed the lessons of this crisis in terms of how they conduct their businesses.

The fact is every American—from Main Street to Wall Street—has a stake in our financial system. Wall Street banks and firms invest the capital that makes it possible for start-ups to sell new products. They provide loans to businesses to expand and to hire. They back mortgages for families purchasing a new home. That's why we'll all stand to gain from these reforms. We all win when investors around the world have confidence in our markets. We all win when shareholders have more power and more information. We all win when consumers are protected against abuse. And we all win when folks are rewarded based on how well they perform, not how well they evade accountability.

In the end, our financial system only works—our market is only free—when there are clear rules and basic safeguards that prevent abuse, that check excess, that ensure that it is more profitable to play by the rules than to game the system. And that's what these reforms are designed to achieve—no more, no less. Because that's how we will ensure that our economy works for consumers, that it works for investors, that it works for financial institutions—that it works for all of us.

This is the central lesson not only of this crisis but of our history. Ultimately, there's no dividing line between Main Street and Wall Street. We rise or fall together as one nation. So these reforms will help lift our economy and lead all of us to a stronger, more prosperous future.

Financial Reforms Are Under Way to Make the US Financial System Stronger

Timothy F. Geithner

Timothy F. Geithner is the US Secretary of the Treasury.

Last month, President [Barack] Obama signed into law reforms that will reshape the American financial system and restore it to its core purpose of generating lasting economic growth.

Today, I want to outline the next steps for financial reform and the challenges we face in making these reforms a success.

But before I do, I think it's worth recalling how we got here.

An Obligation to Reform the Financial System

Reform was an obligation, never a choice.

We had an obligation to fix the basic flaws in our financial system that helped trigger the worst global economic crisis since the Great Depression.

We had an obligation to make sure that this great recession would be remembered not just for the deep damage it caused but also for the sweeping change it compelled.

We had an obligation to rebuild our financial system so it could, once again, be an engine for economic growth and innovation.

The battle for financial reform, while hard fought, was a battle of necessity.

For much of the last century, the American financial system was the envy of the world.

Timothy F. Geithner, "Rebuilding the American Financial System," U.S. Department of the Treasury, August 2, 2010.

Our system provided investors with the strongest protections in the world. Those protections, and our dynamic, competitive market for financial innovation, fueled the global ascendance of American business.

Our system provided the financing that created the great American manufacturing companies; that unleashed a revolution in technology; that led to life-saving advancements in science.

And our system provided hundreds of thousands of engineers and entrepreneurs, scientists and small businesses with an unparalleled opportunity to transform their ideas into industries.

Where the American economy excelled relative to other major developed economies—in innovation and in higher productivity growth—it did so, in part, because our financial system was better at directing investment towards the companies and industries where the returns would be highest.

Now, the American financial system achieved all this because we had a strong set of rules governing finance. These regulatory checks and balances helped create a remarkably long period of relative economic stability. Recessions happened, but they were shorter and less damaging. We appeared to have achieved a system that was reasonably stable, but also very good at innovation.

But over time those great strengths of our financial system were undermined. The careful mix of protections we created eventually eroded.

New industries of consumer finance and mortgage lending grew up outside the banking sector, evading rules necessary to protect consumers. Huge amounts of risk moved outside the banking system to where it was easier to increase leverage.

That, combined with a long period of low real interest rates around the world, led to a race to the bottom in underwriting standards and credit terms. And, ultimately, it led the

American financial system—once the model of efficiency—to misallocate hundreds of billions of dollars towards an unsustainable real estate boom.

When things fell apart, the damage spread far beyond Wall Street. Housing prices fell off a cliff. Business and trade halted around the world. Trillions of dollars in savings vanished. Millions of jobs were lost. And thousands of companies across main street America collapsed.

How did this happen? The failures were many.

On Wall Street and across the American financial system, financial firms of all types took on risks they did not fully understand.

The reforms that are now the law of the land will help us rebuild a pro-growth, pro-investment financial system.

In Washington, financial regulators did not sufficiently use the authority they had to protect consumers and limit excessive risk; policy makers did not act early enough to overhaul a broken system; and Congress legislated loopholes that allowed large parts of the financial industry to operate without oversight, transparency, or restraint.

And, it is important to remember this. In communities across the country, many Americans took on more debt than they could afford and took on financial risks they did not fully appreciate.

We share responsibility for the crisis, and we share responsibility for reform.

Rebuilding a Prosperous Financial System

The reforms that are now the law of the land will help us rebuild a pro-growth, pre-investment financial system; a system that will allow Americans to save for retirement and to borrow to finance an education or a home knowing that proper safeguards are in place to prevent firms from taking advantage of them; a system that will help businesses finance growth with less risk that they will be starved for credit the next time we face an economic downturn.

Now, to get there, we have different responsibilities.

For the American people, the core challenge is to save a larger share of income, to borrow more responsibly, and to be sure we better understand the risks involved in investing and borrowing.

That process is under way.

Americans are rediscovering the importance of living within their means. They're saving more and paying down debt. And they're growing more careful about how they borrow and how they invest. These changes are necessary and healthy. And they will make us stronger as a country.

For the financial industry, your core challenge is to restore the trust and confidence of the American people and your customers and investors around the world.

You will have to make your own decisions about how best to do that, but, I thought, given that I'm here in New York, I'd offer a few suggestions as an interested observer.

Don't wait for Washington to draft every rule before you start changing how you do business.

Get ahead of the process and out in front of your competitors.

Find new ways to improve disclosure for your consumers. End hidden fees. Don't push people into loans they can't afford.

Demonstrate to your business customers—small and large—that after running for cover during the peak of the crisis you are ready and willing to take a chance on them again.

Change how you pay your executives so you are not rewarding them for taking risks that could threaten the stability of the financial system.

Make sure you have board members who understand your business and the risks you are taking.

And, focus on improving your financial position so that your financial ratings, your cost of capital, the amount you have to pay to borrow, all reflect your own financial strength and earnings prospects, not the false expectation that the government will be there in the future to rescue you.

You can do all of that right now, even before the first new rule of financial reform is written.

But a substantial part of the responsibility for reform, of course, falls on Washington.

Those of us in government—policy makers, regulators, and supervisors—must make sure that these reforms meet the promise of the law; that these reforms provide both the necessary protections against financial excess and the benefits of financial innovation.

That is our core challenge.

Principles of Reform

And I want to briefly lay out some of the principles that will guide our work going forward.

First, we have an obligation of speed.

We will move as quickly as possible to bring clarity to the new rules of finance. The rule-writing process traditionally has moved at a frustrating, glacial pace. We must change that.

Second, we will provide full transparency and disclosure.

The regulatory agencies will consult broadly as they write new rules. Draft rules will be published. The public will have a chance to comment. And those comments will be available for everyone to see.

Third, we will not simply layer new rules on top of old, outdated ones.

Everyone that is part of the financial system—the regulated and regulators—knows that we have accumulated layers of rules that can be overwhelming, and these failures of regulation were in some ways as appalling as the failures produced where regulation was absent.

So alongside our efforts to strengthen and improve protections for the economy, we will eliminate rules that did not work. Wherever possible, we will streamline and simplify.

Fourth, we will not risk killing the freedom for innovation that is necessary for economic growth.

Our system allowed too much freedom for predation, abuse and excess risk, but as we put in place rules to correct for those mistakes, we have to strive to achieve a careful balance and safeguard the freedom, competition and innovation that are essential for growth.

Fifth, we will make sure we have a more level playing field—not just between banks and non-banks here in the United States—but also between our financial institutions and those in Europe, Japan, China, and emerging markets who are all competing to finance global growth and development. We will do this by setting high global standards and blocking a 'race to the bottom' from taking place outside the United States.

Finally, we will bring more order and coordination to the regulatory process, so that the agencies responsible for building these reforms are working together, not against each other. This requires us to look carefully at the overall interaction of regulations designed by different regulators and assess the overall burden they present relative to the benefits they offer.

So those are the principles that will guide our implementation of financial reform.

You should hold us accountable for honoring them.

Complicated Reforms

Now, this process is very broad in scope and very complicated. It will take time.

It involves appointing new champions of consumer financial protection and leaders of bank supervision. It involves writing new rules in some of the most complex areas of modern finance. It involves consolidating authority now spread across multiple agencies. It involves setting up new institutions for coordination, crisis management, consumer protection, and for indentifying systemic risks. It involves negotiations with countries around the world.

Each of the agencies involved in implementing financial reform—Treasury, the Federal Reserve [or the Fed, the nation's central bank], the SEC [U.S. Securities and Exchange Commission, which regulates the security industry], the CFTC [U.S. Commodity Futures Trading Commission, which regulates futures trading], the OCC [Office of the Comptroller of the Currency], the FDIC [Federal Deposit Insurance Corporation, which insures bank deposits up to $100,000] and others—are in the process of outlining how they propose to prioritize the rules they now have to write and setting initial dates for when the public will be able to comment on draft rules.

And in September, when the Financial Stability Oversight Council first meets, we will establish an integrated road map for the first stages of reform and put that in the public domain.

Now, without getting ahead of that process, let me provide you with a brief introduction to the steps we expect to take in four of the most important areas over the next several months.

First, consumer protection.

We want to move quickly to give consumers simpler disclosures for credit cards, auto loans, and mortgages, so that they can make better choices, borrow more responsibly, and compare costs.

One of the ways we intend to do that is by combining the two separate and inconsistent federal mortgage disclosure forms that consumers currently get. Next month, we'll convene mortgage companies, consumer advocates, housing counselors, and other experts to gather ideas on how to do that. We'll take the best ones, test them on consumers, and then soon be able to unveil a new, easy to understand, federal disclosure form.

In addition, we will be inviting public comment on new national underwriting standards for mortgages, so that we can begin to shape the reforms of the mortgage market.

Now, consumer protection also requires better enforcement, particularly of consumer finance companies not regulated as banks. And so—building on our very successful effort to stop mortgage scams led by a joint task force we created with the Justice Department and State Attorneys General—we are going to coordinate a national enforcement effort targeted at other forms of consumer abuse, including those financial companies that target members of the military and their families. While our soldiers protect our nation abroad, their families should not be exposed to financial abuse at home.

Second, we are moving forward on reforming the GSEs [government-sponsored enterprises, financial services corporations created by the federal government] and our broader housing finance system.

Later this month, we will bring together at the Treasury Department leading academic experts, consumer and community organizations, industry participants, and other stakeholders for a conference of experts focused on the future of housing finance. We'll use the conference to explore various models of reform and we will seek input from across the political and ideological spectrum.

All financial crises are, at their core, caused by excess leverage, a term we use to describe the amount of risk firms take relative to the financial reserves they hold against those risks.

Chairman [Barney] Frank plans a series of hearings on housing finance reform this fall. And we are required to submit our plan for reform by January of next year [2011].

Third, we are going to move quickly to begin shaping reforms of the derivatives market. To start the process, we will work with the Fed, the SEC, and the CFTC to outline specific quantitative targets for moving the standardized part of the over-the-counter derivatives business onto central clearing-houses. And we must accelerate the international effort to define common global standards for transparency, oversight, and the prevention of manipulation and abuse of these critically important markets.

Constraining Risk Taking

Now, the final area of reform that I want to talk about is perhaps the most important, establishing new rules to constrain risk taking by—and leverage in—the largest global financial institutions.

All financial crises are, at their core, caused by excess leverage, a term we use to describe the amount of risk firms take relative to the financial reserves they hold against those risks.

Capital requirements determine the amount of loss firms can absorb, the magnitude of the risks they can take without risking failure. They help the market provide discipline by forcing shareholders who enjoy profits in good times to be exposed to losses in bad times.

Capital requirements are the financial equivalent of having speed limits on our highways, antilock brakes and airbags in our cars, and building codes in communities prone to earthquakes.

Part of what made this crisis so severe was that capital requirements failed to keep up with risks and failed to force firms to prepare for the possibility of a very severe recession with a substantial reduction in house prices.

This mistake was made worse by the fact that we allowed a large parallel financial system—composed of investment banks, consumer finance companies, and firms like AIG [American International Group, Inc.]—to grow up alongside the regulated banking system. In that parallel system, firms were allowed to operate with very thin capital cushions, and to finance their activities with short-term, unstable sources of funding.

Meanwhile, elsewhere in the world, the rules were in some ways even weaker. That was true in the U.K. [United Kingdom] where—in order to attract business away from New York and Frankfurt [Germany]—they built a financial system on the unstable foundation of a strategy called "light touch regulation." And that was true in many of the other major developed economies where the rules allowed firms to operate with much lower levels of capital relative to risk.

The global capital framework we had in place ahead of this crisis obviously did not work. And we are moving quickly, across the world, to fix it.

Let me describe the key elements of the international agreement we are working to build.

First, we are going to make sure that financial firms hold a lot more capital than they did before the crisis. We want the new requirements to be set so that we could face a crisis of this severity in the future without the government having to step in and provide emergency life support. The major banks will be required to hold enough capital so they could withstand losses similar to what we saw in the depths of this recession and still have the ability to operate without turning to the taxpayer for help.

Second, we are going to make sure that firms meet these requirements with common equity so that they can better absorb losses. In contrast to the rules prevailing today, which allow a wide range of other forms of capital, the requirements will be set in terms of real common equity, tightly defined to mean capital that will truly absorb first losses when firms get into trouble.

Third, firms will be required to hold significantly more capital against the types of risky trading-related assets and obligations that caused so much unexpected financial damage during the crisis.

Fourth, bigger firms and more complex, interconnected firms will have to hold relatively more capital than smaller firms. The largest and most interconnected firms cause more damage when they fail, so they need to hold more capital against risk. That is based on a principle of fairness and also provides incentives for firms to limit their size and reduce their leverage.

And fifth, new capital requirements will be supplemented with new global standards for liquidity management, so that firms can withstand a severe shock in liquidity without deepening the crisis by, for example, selling assets in a panic or cutting credit lines indiscriminately or needlessly turning to central banks for liquidity support—all of which can undermine financial confidence in periods of stress.

Under the framework now being built, firms will be subject to two tiers of capital requirements.

All firms will need to hold a substantial minimum level of capital. And they will be required to hold an added buffer of capital set above the minimum. If a firm suffers losses that force it to eat into that buffer, it will have to raise capital, reduce dividends, or suspend share repurchases.

This will help make the system more stable over time, in part by forcing banks to move more quickly to strengthen their balance sheets as the risk of potential losses increases.

Now, the most consequential part of this framework will be the new quantitative capital ratios.

We know they need to be substantially higher than they were. But we also know that if we set them too high too fast, we could hurt economic recovery or simply end up pushing risk outside of the banking system, something that could ultimately come back to haunt us.

To limit that potential, we plan to give banks a reasonable transition period.

Banks will have until the beginning of 2013 to meet the new minimum, and will have several years beyond that to build up their new capital buffers while implementing a progressively more stringent definition of what counts as capital. Importantly, that means banks will have the opportunity to meet these new requirements in part through future earnings and that will help protect the recovery currently under way.

For the U.S. financial system, it is important to note that because we moved so quickly, with the bank stress tests in early 2009, to force banks to raise more common equity, our financial system is in a very strong position internationally to adapt to the new global rules.

Reshaping the Financial System

Now, as I said at the start, enacting Wall Street reform was a hard-fought battle.

And the opponents of reform will continue to claim—as they have over the past year—that these reforms will bring about the end of American enterprise.

Well, let me provide some perspective.

Eight decades ago, a previous generation of Americans battled through a great depression. And four years after the great crash of 1929, they rose to meet the great challenge of their day by establishing bold new bank protections and new securities laws.

At the time, just as now, the opponents of reform predicted grave danger.

In 1933, *Time* magazine wrote, in reference to the bill that created the FDIC, "through the great banking houses of Manhattan last week ran wild-eyed alarm. Big bankers stared at one another in anger and astonishment. A bill just passed. . . would rivet upon their institutions what they considered a monstrous system. . . such a system, they felt, would not only rob them of their pride of profession but would reduce all U.S. banking to its lowest level."

A year later, in 1934, the President of the Chamber of Commerce, speaking of the Securities Exchange Act said, "it is the opinion not only of Stock Exchange brokers, but of thoughtful businessmen that its sweeping and drastic provisions would seriously affect the legitimate business of all members of Stock Exchanges and investment banks, with resultant disastrous consequences to the stock market; would greatly prejudice the interest of all investors; would tend to destroy the liquidity of banks and would impose on corporations of the country serious handicaps in the practical operation of their business."

The reforms we passed will fundamentally reshape the entire financial system.

Notwithstanding those fears and distortions, the reforms that followed the Great Depression laid the foundation for decades of prosperity and led to one of the most impressive records of investment, innovation and growth any major economy had ever seen.

Financial reform cannot just be about fighting the last war. Future risks will look different than those we've seen in the past. And so we need a system that is more adaptable and resilient; one that builds a strong foundation for lasting economic growth.

The reforms we passed will fundamentally reshape the entire financial system. They will require financial firms to change the way they do business, to change the way they treat customers, to change the way they manage risk, and to change the way they reward their executives.

These reforms will be tough, but they will be toughest on those who took the greatest risks; on those who operated closest to the edge of prudence; on those who chased the market down and competed in a race to the bottom in standards and practices; and on those who made [the] most of their profits in the most unsustainable of ways.

And these reforms will benefit American business and the American people, by providing a more stable source of financing for the investments that will drive future gains in income and future growth.

Now, I know that some of you here today are students at this great university.

You have come of age at a time of great national challenge. And, while I know it hasn't been easy, because of that, you will bring to the world not just a greater appreciation for risk and responsibility, but also a recognition that what we bring to the world depends not so much on how much we earn, but on the nature of the work we do. That is a good thing.

America is coming back. The economy is healing. We are repairing the damage caused by the crisis. And we are taking the hard steps now, by implementing reforms that will be essential to our capacity to grow and prosper in the future.

Financial reform will make our financial system stronger, and it will make our economy stronger.

CHAPTER 3

Will the *Citizens United* Decision Lead to More Government Corruption?

Overview: The Supreme Court, the First Amendment, and Government Corruption

Lela Gray

Lela Gray is a Government Law Review member.

The U.S. Supreme Court (Supreme Court) decision in the case *Citizens United v. Federal Election Commission* is causing fireworks throughout the nation weeks after New Years. In a heavily split 5–4 decision, the Supreme Court held that the First Amendment prohibits Congress from barring corporate and union general funds to support or oppose political candidates. Disclaimer and disclosure requirements, however, do not offend the First Amendment.

Court watchers had the outcome of this case already predicted—that Chief Justice [John] Roberts and Justices [Samuel] Alito, [Anthony] Kennedy, [Antonin] Scalia, and [Clarence] Thomas would strike down restrictive corporate campaign spending laws as unconstitutional. Yet, the sharp reactions to the opinion, the ongoing public debate, and the ninety-page dissent written by Justice [John Paul] Stevens seem to signal that this issue is all but settled. So which side is right? Was this judicial activism, or was it a long overdue check against congressional infringement on the most fundamental of our freedoms?

Background

Congress has prohibited corporations from giving money directly to federal political candidates for over a century. The Bipartisan Campaign Reform Act of 2002 (Campaign Reform

Lela Gray, "2010's First Landmark Supreme Court Decision: Balancing Potential Political Corruption and Free Speech," *Albany Government Law Review Fireplace*, March 8, 2010. http://aglr.wordpress.com. Reproduced by permission of the publisher and the author.

Act) strengthened this tradition by prohibiting corporations and unions from applying their general treasury funds to pay for any form of media or "electioneering communication" aimed at advocating for the election or defeat of a candidate in certain federal elections. An "electioneering communication" is defined as "any broadcast, cable, or satellite communication" referring to an identifiable candidate for federal office, and which is "publicly distributed" within thirty days of a primary or sixty days of a general election.

Citizens United (Citizens) is a conservative nonprofit advocacy corporation with an annual budget of $12 million, most of which is derived from individual donations with a small portion stemming from contributions by for-profit corporations. In January 2008, Citizens released a ninety-minute documentary entitled *Hillary: The Movie*, which casts a critical shadow over Hillary Clinton's character and much of her political career. The film was released in theaters and on DVD, but Citizens wanted to advertise the film and make it viewable to cable and satellite subscribers at no charge via video-on-demand. To ensure their ability to do so without fear of criminal penalties under the Campaign Reform Act, the corporation sought declaratory and injunctive relief against the Federal Election Commission (FEC). The District Court held that the Campaign Reform Act was facially constitutional and denied Citizens' request, instead granting summary judgment in favor of the FEC. Citizens then appealed directly to the Supreme Court.

Side 1: This Is About Free Speech

Those who supported Citizens' efforts argue that free speech is a fundamental right that cannot be overcome without a compelling government interest. In their minds, a statutory ban on ads criticizing political candidates is precisely the type of government infringement on free speech that the founders sought to prevent when they wrote the First Amendment.

They also fail to see any compelling government interest served by the ban. They contend that any compelling interest argument put forth by the government is destroyed by the fact that the film can be downloaded online and purchased on DVD—two methods of distribution that are not banned by the Campaign Reform Act. Thus, the purported compelling interest of preventing political corruption by banning the distribution of this politically charged film is destroyed by the fact that the information can be readily obtained in other ways.

President Obama declared that the ruling was a major victory for the oil industry, big banks, and other powerful interest groups that use their loud bankrolls "to drown out the voices of everyday Americans."

Another overarching argument is that this type of censorship is dangerous because it starts a slippery slope that will lead to more and more censorship. For example, why stop at merely banning political ads and campaigning messages on television? Why not ban all of these messages on all forms of media? Does the Campaign Reform Act do that already? The majority made it clear that these questions are representative of their fears. These were the types of questions thrown at the government over and over again. During oral arguments, members of the Court seemingly pinned the government's lawyer in the uncomfortable position of having to defend book banning in order to support the law banning the use of corporate funds in electioneering ads. The government tried to wiggle out of this corner, but ultimately fell right into the trap and admitted that the Campaign Reform Act could not only ban certain books but could also ban signs with political messages if those signs were paid for by corporate treasury funds. In fact, the government seemed to get distracted by these questions and failed to focus on larger, more convincing arguments that supported its side.

Side 2: This Is About Potential Political Corruption

"We are moving to an age where we won't have the senator from Arkansas or the congressman from North Carolina, but the senator from Wal-Mart and the congressman from Bank of America."

The rationale behind the century-old laws prohibiting corporations from directly giving money to political candidates is easily understood—as a country, we do not want big business buying seats in Congress for their pet politicians. Surely the government has a compelling interest in keeping corruption out of its offices. Some have warned that easing restrictions would be a "potential step towards the formation of a corporatocracy—a system of governance where corporations use their power to influence the will of nations."

A more modern argument in favor of corporate political contribution regulation is that without laws like the Campaign Reform Act, stockholders may have money they invested in a corporation being used for political advocacy they oppose. By invalidating laws like these, the court "clear[s] the way for the nation's largest for-profit corporations to electioneer with general treasuries amassed from investors who did not intend the money be used for political purposes and who will not likely obtain relief."

President [Barack] Obama declared that the ruling was a major victory for the oil industry, big banks, and other powerful interest groups that use their loud bankrolls "to drown out the voices of everyday Americans." The president promised to collaborate with Congress to craft a legislative response.

Supreme Court Decision and Rationale

Right off the bat the Court dispersed with the narrower arguments of both sides because a narrowly tailored opinion in this case would mean a case-by-case determination of similar issues in the future. Instead, the Court rolled up their sleeves, so to speak, and noted that "judicial responsibility" required a consideration of the facial validity of § 441b. This declaration was shocking to many who never thought the Supreme Court would go this far. Perhaps no one was more shocked than the dissenters, led by Justice Stevens.

Justice Stevens sharply criticized the holding as violating the vitals of *stare decisis*, seeing no difference in the arguments made in *Citizens* and the arguments made in the *Austin [v. Michigan Chamber of Commerce]* and *McConnell [v. Federal Election Commission]* cases. Before *Citizens*, the functional equivalency test was the standard. Under the functional equivalency test, the question was whether a communication posed a risk of corruption to the election process so great that Congress was compelled to regulate it. Justice Stevens would have kept that test, but the majority has overruled him and the test. Frustrated, Stevens noted that "[t]he only relevant thing that has changed since *Austin* and *McConnell* is the composition of this Court." Stevens is right about the huge difference in the Court's composition; he is the one and only remaining member of the *Austin* majority.

So Which Side Is Right?

Right or wrong, it seems clear to this author that judicial activism was steering the boat in this case. Almost all of Citizens' arguments were narrowly tailored to argue that *Hillary* should not fall within the reach of 441b rather than arguing that § 441b is unconstitutional as a whole. Thus, the Court could have decided this case on narrower issues and avoided holding § 441b facially unconstitutional, but they chose instead to go for the jugular.

By holding this law facially invalid, the Court has begun to rewind over a century of legal precedent aimed at preventing government corruption via corporate buyout (or buy-in). There is now a real cause for concern that corporations will soon be permitted to openly buy voting power by spending millions on campaigns to promote preferred candidates and smear opposing runners. While we may now be subjected to political smear campaign ads, our right to curse and publicly proclaim our disagreement with the political pet candidate in the ad will be protected as well.

The US Supreme Court Has Upheld Institutional Government Corruption

Aminu Gamawa

Aminu Gamawa is a master of laws student at Harvard Law School from Nigeria.

What started as a 90-minute political campaign documentary against then-presidential candidate Hillary Clinton ended in the Supreme Court with a decision that was described by some critics as one of the worst since *Dred Scott* [*Dred Scott v. Sandford*, an 1857 Supreme Court decision that held African American slaves were not protected by the U.S. Constitution and could not be U.S. citizens]. *Hillary: The Movie* was produced by Citizens United, a conservative nonprofit, as part of its campaign against the former Democratic presidential aspirant, and was released during the Democratic presidential primaries in 2008.

The judgment, which relaxes the restriction on power of the corporations to directly spend on advertising during federal elections, was described by Harvard law professor Lawrence Lessig as "proverbial fuel on the fire." He notes that the issue is not whether corporations are silenced or their First Amendment right to free speech [is] upheld. More importantly, the outcome is an assault on democracy, capable of promoting a system that will further erode the public trust in their elected officers. Lessig cautioned that [the] decision would undermine the participation of the citizens in the democratic process and that it gives unfair advantage to corporations, whose financial prowess will give them a stronger voice than the electorate.

Aminu Gamawa, "*Citizens United* Upholds Institutional Corruption," *Harvard Law Record*, January 28, 2010. www.hlrecord.org. Reproduced by permission.

The Framers' Concern About Corruption

Lessig heads Harvard's [Edmond J.] Safra Center for Ethics, which studies the intersection between politics, interest groups and corruption in the U.S. politics. As part of the reading for a course convened by the program, I came across a very interesting article by an expert on political corruption, Zephyr Rain Teachout . . . which I found very relevant to the Court's decision in *Citizens United*.

Teachout writes that the Framers of the Constitution were obsessed with corruption and saw it as one of the greatest threats to democracy. They designed the system in such a way that corrupt leaders will not only lose their positions, but also their reputation. The Founding Fathers built mechanisms into the Constitution to safeguard democracy by ensuring transparency, accountability and citizens' participation in the political process. The independence of the political officeholders from other special interests was of paramount importance to the Framers.

History has shown that when leaders put their self-interest above those who elected them, it . . . inevitably leads to collapse of the democratic system.

Teachout writes that "corruption was discussed more often in the constitutional convention than factions, violence, or instability. It was a topic of concern on almost a quarter of the days that the members convened. [James] Madison recorded the specific term corruption fifty-four times, and the vast majority of the corruption discussions were spearheaded by influential delegates Madison, [Robert] Morris [Jr.], [George] Mason, and [James] Wilson. The attendees were concerned about the corrupting influence of wealth, greed, and ambition." It is not an overstatement to say that the Framers actually saw the Constitution as an instrument to fight corruption.

The Framers defined political corruption to include "self-serving use of public power for private ends, including, without limitation, bribery, public decisions to serve private wealth made because of dependent relationships, public decisions to serve executive power made because of dependent relationships, and use by public officials of their positions of power to become wealthy."

Their efforts to curb corruption in the political process is visible in issues including the regulation of elections, term limits, limits on holding multiple offices, limitations on accepting foreign gifts, the veto power, the impeachment clause, and provisions for the separation of powers, among other measures, with a view to ensure that leaders represent the interest of their constituency and not personal interests. In the words of Teachout, "taking seriously the architecture [of the Constitution] requires more than passing knowledge of what motivated the choice of architecture. Political corruption is context without which other specific words don't make sense; it is embodied in the text itself through other words that can't be understood without understanding corruption."

Ignoring the threat of corruption to democracy is . . . a serious problem that cannot be taken lightly.

Undermining Public Trust in Government

History has shown that when leaders put their self-interest above those who elected them, it undermines the trust of the people in the process and inevitably leads to collapse of the democratic system. The Roman and Greek empires are classic examples. The danger of democracies leaving political corruption unchecked is succinctly captured by Teachout: "voters will stop voting, people will stop running for office, and citizens will stop making serious efforts to read news and understand the public issues of their day, because they will believe that such efforts are futile," she writes.

In *McConnell v. Federal Election Commission*, 540 U.S. 93, which the Court overturned in *Citizens United v. Federal Election Commission*, the Court had made the following powerful comments:

"Just as troubling to a functioning democracy as classic quid pro quo corruption is the danger that officeholders will decide issues not on the merits or the desires of their constituencies, but according to the wishes of those who have made large financial contributions valued by the officeholder. Even if it occurs only occasionally, the potential for such undue influence is manifest. And unlike straight cash-for-votes transactions, such corruption is neither easily detected nor practical to criminalize. The best means to prevention is to identify and remove the temptation."

Ignoring the threat of corruption to democracy is, therefore, a serious problem that cannot be taken lightly. I agree with Teachout when she writes that "internal decay of our political life due to power-and-wealth seeking by representatives and elites is a major and constant threat to our democracy. History provides some powerful tools to allow us [to] incorporate the anticorruption principle into the constitutional law of democracy. We should pay attention to it." The recent decision of the Supreme Court ignores this history, undermining the Constitution's efforts to curb corruption at the highest level.

The 5–4 conservative majority decision was delivered by Justice Anthony Kennedy '61, and concurred in by Justice Samuel Alito, Chief Justice John Roberts '79, Justice Clarence Thomas and Justice Antonin Scalia '60. Justice Sonia Sotomayor began her Supreme Court career with a dissent. She joined three other liberal justices in disagreeing with the majority decision. The dissenting judgment delivered by Justice [John Paul] Stevens severely criticized the majority court for ignoring the dangerous consequence of the decision on democracy:

"At bottom, the Court's opinion is thus a rejection of the common sense of the American people, who have recognized a need to prevent corporations from undermining self-government since the founding, and who have fought against the distinctive corrupting potential of corporate electioneering since the days of Theodore Roosevelt. It is a strange time to repudiate that common sense. While American democracy is imperfect, few outside the majority of this Court would have thought its flaws included a dearth of corporate money in politics," Justice Stevens wrote.

A Victory for Special Interests

The decision overruled a decade of precedent laid down in *McConnell*, a 2003 decision that upheld the part of the Bipartisan Campaign Reform Act of 2002, which restricted campaign spending by corporations and unions, as well as *Austin v. Michigan Chamber of Commerce*, 494 U.S. 652, a 1990 decision that upheld restrictions on corporate spending to support or oppose political candidates.

Citizens United *has introduced a new era in the U.S. politics.*

In his weekly address on Saturday [January 23, 2010], President Barack Obama '91 criticized the decision as "a huge victory to the special interests and their lobbyists." The president expressed his disappointment with the ruling, saying that he could not "think of anything more devastating to the public interest. The last thing we need to do is hand more influence to the lobbyists in Washington, or more power to the special interests to tip the outcome of elections." He noted that even foreign corporations would now have say in U.S. politics; candidates that disagreed with corporations would come under serious attack from the corporations during election.

Obama went on to observe that "all of us, regardless of party, should be worried that it will be that much harder to get fair, commonsense financial reforms, or close unwarranted tax loopholes that reward corporations from sheltering their income or shipping American jobs offshore." He also cautioned that the decision makes it "more difficult to pass commonsense laws" to promote energy independence or expand health care.

The danger is clear!

Undermining Democracy

The competition will now be intense among the corporations to producing the highest number of Senators and Representatives. Doesn't this undermine the role of the public in the American democracy? Can individuals' contributions to candidates now count in the campaign process? Will this be the last Congress that is truly elected by the people? How much would this decision contribute in promoting institutional corruption? I am sure most politicians will be more concerned about pleasing the corporations than their constituencies. It will be dangerous for any of them to fall out with the corporations.

[The decision in Citizens United*] is an assault on democracy and negation of the text and original understanding of the Constitution as understood by the Founding Fathers.*

American democracy has been a model to many countries across the globe. But the recent decision by the Supreme Court legalizing direct corporate participation which overturns a time-revered restriction on the corporation is a worrisome development that deserves concern of anyone that is interested in American democracy's future. *Citizens United* has introduced a new era in the U.S. politics.

The Constitution's "We the People" has gradually become "We the Corporations." Equating corporations with human beings undoubtedly undermines the participation of individual citizens in the political process. Election into political office under the new regime will largely depend on having the highest donation from the corporations. Corporations and their interests, which sometimes include interests of foreign nationals, will now have the strongest voice in the U.S. politics.

It will not be surprising to see Blackwater, Wal-Mart, Exxon and other corporations being better represented in Congress than citizens, whose interest and participation the Constitution seeks to preserve. This is an unwelcome development that anyone concerned about preserving the U.S.'s long-cherished democracy must oppose.

The matter of democratic integrity, transparency and accountability transcends the usual liberal/conservative or Democrat/Republican divide. It is an assault on democracy and negation of the text and original understanding of the Constitution as understood by the Founding Fathers, who strived to craft a document that would preserve democracy by protecting the interest of the electorate over and above other interests.

One might ask if there is anything Congress can do. Even before the decision was announced, an advocacy group called Change Congress was working to pursue the passage of a bipartisan bill called the Fair Elections Now Act. The bill is sponsored by congressmen Sens. Dick Durbin (D-IL) and Arlen Specter (R-PA), and Reps. John Larson (D-CT) and Walter Jones (R-NC).

"Under this legislation, congressional candidates who raise a threshold number of small-dollar donations would qualify for a chunk of funding—several hundred thousand dollars for House, millions for many Senate races. If they accept this funding, they can't raise big-dollar donations. But they can raise contributions up to $100, which would be matched four to one by a central fund. A reduced fee for TV airtime is also an element of this bill. This would create an incentive for politicians to opt into this system and run people-powered campaigns."

President Obama said that he has instructed his advisers to work with Congress on a forceful, bipartisan response. In a *New York Times* op-ed, David D. Kirkpatrick wrote that because of the enormous threat of this decision to democracy, some members of Congress are working hard to introduce new laws that will, cure the defect by either

- Imposing a ban [on] political advertising by corporations that hire lobbyists, receive government money, or collect most of their revenue abroad;

- Tightening rules against coordination between campaigns and outside groups so that, for example, they could not hire the same advertising firms or consultants; or

- Requiring shareholder approval of political expenditures, or even forcing chief executives to appear as sponsors of commercials their companies pay for.

What is really necessary . . . , as Professor Lessig puts it, is an alternative, "Not the alternative that tries to silence any speaker but an alternative that allows us to believe once again that our government is guided by reason or judgment or even just the politics of the people in a district and not by the need to raise money."

The Supreme Court Weakened the Definition of Government Corruption

Heather K. Gerken

Heather K. Gerken is a professor of law at Yale Law School and an expert in election law.

Yesterday the Supreme Court struck down the federal ban on corporate independent expenditures in *Citizens United v. [Federal Election Commission]*. Before *Citizens United*, corporations were not allowed to spend money from their general treasuries to call for the election or defeat of federal candidates close to Election Day, even if they did so without consulting with the candidate. In striking down the federal ban, the Supreme Court overruled two of its decisions: *Austin v. Michigan Chamber of Commerce*, decided in 1990, and *McConnell v. [Federal Election Commission]*, decided less than 7 years ago.

Howls of Protest

The decision has been met with howls of protest from reformers: The Supreme Court overruled its own precedent! A century-long tradition of regulation is in jeopardy! Corporations will flood the airwaves and further corrupt our already corrupt political process! It's "a disaster for the American people," says Fred Wertheimer of the campaign finance reform organization Democracy 21.

It's not surprising that reformers are outraged. *Austin* has long been the darling of reformers; it's as close as the Court has ever come to saying Congress can regulate campaign fi-

Heather K. Gerken, "The Real Problem with *Citizens United*," *The American Prospect Online*, January 22, 2010. http://www.prospect.org. The American Prospect, 1710 Rhode Island Avenue, NW, 12th Floor, Washington, DC 20036. All rights reserved. Reprinted with permission from Heather Gerken.

nance to promote "equality." Reformers have long argued that reform should level the playing field between the monied and the everyday citizen. The Court, however, has generally disagreed. It has repeatedly rejected the equality rationale and, with the exception of *Austin*, insisted that preventing corruption is the only legitimate grounds for regulation.

If the Court rigidly insists that Congress can regulate only to prevent quid-pro-corruption, narrowly defined, then Citizens United *has implications that extend well beyond what corporations can do.*

Still, as a practical matter, the opinion is just one more step in the direction the Court was already heading. As Nate Persily, director of the Center for Law and Politics at Columbia points out, earlier cases had already substantially limited Congress's power to restrict independent corporate expenditures; *Citizens United* was just the last nail in the coffin. The real damage to the cause of reform came earlier, with cases that made less of a splash but probably mattered more. An earlier case, for instance, licensed corporations to run independent ads attacking or supporting candidates provided they stopped just short of telling us how to vote. As a practical matter, there's not much distance between an ad that tells voters to "call Senator X and tell her to stop being mean to puppies" and one that tells voters to "vote against Senator X." Moreover, whatever the reform community thought of *Austin*, Supreme Court observers have long thought *Austin* was a goner. Even the Solicitor General was unwilling to defend the decision's equality rationale.

Limiting the Definition of Corruption

The truth is that the most important line in the decision was not the one overruling *Austin*. It was this one: "ingratiation and access . . . are not corruption." For many years, the Court

had gradually expanded the corruption rationale to extend beyond quid pro quo corruption (donor dollars for legislative
votes). It had licensed Congress to regulate even when the
threat was simply that large donors had better access to politicians or that politicians had become "too compliant with
the[ir] wishes." Indeed, at times the Court went so far as to
say that even the mere *appearance* of "undue influence" or the
public's "cynical assumption that large donors call the tune"
was enough to justify regulation. "Ingratiation and access," in
other words, *were* corruption as far as the Court was concerned. Justice [Anthony] Kennedy didn't say that the Court
was overruling these cases. But that's just what it did.

If the Court rigidly insists that Congress can regulate only
to prevent quid-pro-corruption, narrowly defined, then *Citizens United* has implications that extend well beyond what
corporations can do. Justice Kennedy's own opinion even
hints at the possibility, as he notes that the evidence supporting the "soft money" limits—which apply across the board—
rests on evidence about the connection between money and
political access. While Justice Kennedy backed off from saying
anything definitive, we may find that it was the Court's discussion of corruption, not corporations, that matters most in
the long run.

The *Citizens United* Ruling Will Increase Corruption in the US Government

David P. Hamilton

David P. Hamilton is a political activist in Austin, Texas.

The primary political story of this year's midterm election flows from the Supreme Court's recent *Citizens United v. Federal Election Commission* decision. This 5–4 decision held that corporate funding of independent political broadcasts in candidate elections cannot be limited under the First Amendment.

A Flood of Corporate Money

The already apparent result has been that millions of corporate dollars are flowing into the campaigns nationwide attacking Democrats. Sheila Krumholz of the Center for Responsive Politics predicts "$3.7 billion will be spent on this midterm election," up 30% from the last midterm election. Spending on political ads has increased 75% compared to the 2008 presidential election year.

This flood of ungoverned cash is only just beginning. Increasingly, these contributions are being made anonymously with impunity. Karl Rove now controls a campaign fund 10 times larger than that of the Republican National Committee, 95% of it from three militantly right-wing billionaires. The Chamber of Commerce, with 300,000 members, has raised a huge political fund and spent $28 million, largely from just 45 members, $7 million from "Swiftboat" Bob Perry of Houston [who made contributions to Swift Vets for Truth, formerly

David P. Hamilton, "The 'Citizens United' Decision and the Terminal Corruption of American Electoral Politics," *The Rag Blog*, October 28, 2010. Theragblog.blogspot.com. Reproduced by permission.

Swift Boat Veterans for Truth, a group that opposed John Kerry's candidacy for the 2004 presidential election].

Under the new rules governing political campaign financing, the capital class hegemony over the upper strata of U.S. government has been institutionalized.

Money coming from outside the country is also involved, but that fact is marginal to the larger issue. Amounts being spent by these political action committees to defeat Democrats are unprecedented. More than ever, elections are a commodity for sale and the price is being driven up so that only the very rich can afford them.

The consensus prediction of the outcome of the upcoming midterm elections is the widespread defeat of Democrats, losing control of the House and possibly the Senate too. This result will be determined primarily by the sad state of the economy and the failure of [President Barack] Obama's leadership.

Dominance of the Capital Ruling Class

However, as a result of *Citizens United* the process has fundamentally changed. The playing field has never been level, but the advantages now enjoyed by the capitalist class in the electoral system have reached a qualitatively new high. The primary advantage of the Right has been unleashed. Under the new rules governing political campaign financing, the capital class hegemony over the upper strata of U.S. government has been institutionalized.

Leftists have always argued that there is a U.S. capitalist ruling class with its power based in its control of the major corporations and that capitalist class money corrupts elections. Because of the lack of public funding and the high costs associated with running for office, big private sector money has long been necessary to be a serious player.

However, in the past there were legal limitations on corporate contributions that allowed non-corporate elements to compete, albeit at a financial disadvantage, usually losing to the better financed candidates. The restrictions that remain are quickly becoming irrelevant and no new ones can be reasonably expected from a government increasingly beholden to corporate capitalist interests.

NPR [National Public Radio] recently reported that one Republican-supporting political action fund, among many, was spending over $100,000 for negative advertising at just one small market newspaper in one closely contested congressional race. That's the new norm. Millions in these funds are currently being spent to defeat progressives like Alan Grayson of Florida. The possibility of public funding of elections coming from politicians in the service of big capitalist interests is slight indeed.

The capitalist ruling class has globalized. They are no longer the U.S. ruling class so much as the largest national sector of an increasingly integrated international ruling class. Capital knows no borders. You can buy any publicly held stock in the world in dozens of stock markets worldwide 24/7. The heretofore essential countervailing sector, labor, has no chance to exert close to an equivalent influence while operating in a national context.

What has changed is the depth and reach of capitalist ruling class control. Like their wealth, their power has grown exponentially; they have increased their range of operation and become internationally integrated in recent years. In the U.S., their control has now become enshrined in the basic law of the land.

In this stagnant democracy where, outside of presidential elections, large majorities don't participate, the Republicans have correctly adopted the Rovian [referring to Karl Rove, the former senior adviser and deputy chief of staff to former president George W. Bush] strategy emphasizing base mobilization rather than appealing to the largely mythical center. Thus, their motivating ideology has become more radically rightist. Disguising their racism as concern for immigration, crime, busing, private education, etc., is their specialty.

Promoting Political Instability

As a silver lining to this dark cloud, it is logical to assume that more people will see the validity of the assertion that democracy in America has been corrupted by corporate money. The socialist Left should grow in the context of imperial decline and political polarization. Never has serious reform looked more improbable and never have the culprits looked so conspicuous.

If elections have become a fraud perpetrated upon the public, is participation in them unprincipled in that it lends credence to this fraud? Should we encourage people to vote for liberal Democrats or Greens or anyone when we know the game is rigged? Must we accept competition on an unlevel playing field on our opponent's home turf with them providing the referees?

Or should we instead be encouraging the refusal to participate in corrupt elections? Is authentic democracy impossible under the current system? Should a primary goal of the Left in the future be to delegitimize this corrupt electoral system? Is that impossible if you participate?

This hypothesis concerning the reach and power of capitalist class control has been substantiated by Obama. Given a unique opportunity to lead toward real change, he has instead proven himself to be just another politician who protects the interests of the capitalist class first and foremost.

During the 2008 presidential campaign, while standing in front of an Austin audience, he repeatedly called himself a "progressive." That was pure pandering. Instead, his administration has expanded American militarism with more money and more U.S. troops fighting in more countries than ever;

has produced a health care "reform" that in no fundamental way reforms health care, that mandates you buy a faulty product in the private sector, and that was written largely by health industry lobbyists; and has passed financial "reform" written by lobbyists for the financial sector and their past executives now working within the Obama administration after first forking over hundreds of billions of your tax dollars to "stimulate" them instead of us.

Obama's administration has failed to curb corporate compensation; has failed to close Guantánamo [Bay, a U.S. detainment facility in Cuba] and has expanded CIA [Central Intelligence Agency] assassination programs that include the targeting of American citizens (later defending the practice in court as a "state secret"); has raided the homes and offices of antiwar leaders and confiscated their records; has failed to help millions faced with foreclosure after promising to do so and has announced it will appeal any court ban on future foreclosures while continuing to bail out investment banks who leveraged up the housing bubble.

This irreconcilable conflict of fundamental interests will promote political instability that will increase as this corruption becomes more glaring, entrenched and widespread.

The administration has shown itself unwilling to pressure Israel to make peace with the Palestinians; has done next to nothing to end the drug war; has allowed environmental disaster in the Gulf [of Mexico] through incompetence and a failure of regulatory oversight and then quickly lifted the ban on deepwater drilling, etc., *ad nauseum.*

Now the Obama Justice Department has successfully appealed the federal judge's ruling that "Don't Ask, Don't Tell" is unconstitutional. Before a national audience this ex-professor of constitutional law achieved his nadir of veracity by arguing that protecting gays from continued oppression by the military was best accomplished by a legislative branch that had only recently refused to do so and where his majority is about to shrink if not disappear.

This was soon followed by news that Obama's "Justice" Department will defend Bush's attorney general, John Ashcroft, against legitimate charges that after 9/11 [September 11, 2001, terrorist attacks on the United States] he ordered Muslim Americans to be held without charges, denied them access to lawyers, and had them carried off to secret prisons and tortured.

Obama's record is only progressive in comparison to reactionary Republicans and its lack of progressivism is the principal reason for the "enthusiasm gap." Next week [in the November 2, 2010, midterm elections], the Republicans will get no more votes nationwide than they got when they were soundly defeated in 2008. However, the Democrats will receive many fewer than 2008. Most of those who have abandoned Barack Obama are to his Left. Meanwhile, most Democrats continue to pursue the outmoded strategy of appealing to moderates.

Of course, merely not voting is an insufficient response. Denouncing the process would be not only truthful but very likely a productive strategic innovation for the Left in the future—to picket polling places, to urge people to deface ballots, to publicly destroy registration cards like Vietnam-era draft cards and to proselytize around the analysis that the electoral system and the politicians it produces are inherently corrupt.

Fundamental reforms that reverse *Citizens United*, ban corporate money from political campaigns altogether, and establish publicly funded elections are reasonable and popular but unachievable goals in the present political context and, hence, revolutionary. This irreconcilable conflict of fundamental interests will promote political instability that will increase as this corruption becomes more glaring, entrenched and widespread.

The *Citizens United* Decision Undermines US Democracy by Legitimizing Corruption

Fred Wertheimer

Fred Wertheimer is president of Democracy 21, a nonprofit, non-partisan organization dedicated to making democracy work for all Americans.

Today's [January 21, 2010] Supreme Court decision in the *Citizens United [v. Federal Election Commission]* case is a disaster for the American people and a dark day for the Supreme Court.

The decision will unleash unprecedented amounts of corporate "influence-seeking" money on our elections and create unprecedented opportunities for corporate "influence-buying" corruption.

Today's decision is the most radical and destructive campaign finance decision in Supreme Court history. In order to reach the decision, five justices abandoned longstanding judicial principles, judicial precedents and judicial restraint.

Favoring Corporations

With the *Citizens United* opinion, Chief Justice [John] Roberts has abandoned the illusory public commitments he made to "judicial modesty" and "respect for precedent" to cast the deciding vote for a radical decision that profoundly undermines our democracy.

In a stark choice between the right of American citizens to a government free from "influence-buying" corruption and

Fred Wertheimer, "Supreme Court Decision in Citizens United Case Is Disaster for American People and Dark Day for the Court," *Democracy 21*, January 21, 2010. Democracy21.org. Reproduced by permission.

the economic and political interests of American corporations, five Supreme Court justices today came down in favor of American corporations.

With a stroke of the pen, five justices wiped out a century of American history devoted to preventing corporate corruption of our democracy.

The radical nature of today's decision can be seen in the fact that the Court is overruling cases decided in 1990, 2003 and 2007, without any changed circumstances to justify these abrupt reversals.

The only change that has occurred is a change in the makeup of the Court itself and that provides no justification for overturning past decisions.

The Supreme Court decision in *Citizens United* is wrong for the country, wrong for the Constitution and wrong for our democracy. It will not stand the test of time or history.

The Supreme Court majority has acted recklessly to free up corporations to use their immense, aggregate corporate wealth to flood federal elections and buy government influence. The *Fortune* 100 companies alone had combined revenues of $13 trillion and profits of $605 billion during the last election cycle.

Under today's decision, insurance companies, banks, drug companies, energy companies and the like will be free to *each* spend $5 million, $10 million or more of corporate funds to elect or defeat a federal candidate—and thereby to buy influence over the candidate's positions on issues of economic importance to the companies.

Today's decision turns back the clock to the nineteenth century, eliminating a national policy to prevent the use of corporate wealth to corrupt government decisions—a policy that has been in existence for more than a century.

Members of Congress have passed and presidents have signed numerous laws over the years to prevent "influence-buying" corruption of our government. These laws have consistently been upheld by the Supreme Court.

Today, five justices issued a decision that will empower "influence-buying" corruption.

In the name of the Constitution, five justices have substituted their pro-corporate policy views for the anti-corruption policy views of the representatives elected by citizens to establish our national policies under our constitutional system of government.

This decision will have a devastating impact on the ability of citizens to believe that *their* government is acting on *their* behalf, instead of advancing the interests of the nation's corporations at their *expense.*

In the coming weeks, Congress should explore all possible legislative options to address the dangerous corruption problems opened up by the Supreme Court today.

The *Citizens United* decision reinforces the need to dramatically increase the role of citizens in financing our elections with small "non-influence-seeking" contributions.

This requires enacting legislation to repair the presidential public financing system and create a new system of congressional public financing, and to make small donors the key players in these systems by providing public funds to match small contributions. Democracy 21 strongly supports such legislation.

Reaching Out to Benefit Corporations

Ironically, the constitutionality of the corporate spending ban was never even raised by the plaintiffs in the lower court consideration of this case. Instead, the justices, in essence, started the case themselves when, on their own, they ordered further briefing and argument on the constitutionality of the corporate spending ban.

Ignoring the longstanding judicial doctrine of constitutional avoidance, the Court majority has reached out to decide *Citizens United* on broad constitutional grounds rather than on the various narrower grounds that were available. If the

Court had made its decision on any of these narrower grounds, it would not have disrupted more than a hundred years of national policy to prevent corporate "influence-buying" corruption.

A *Washington Post* Outlook piece by Bob Kaiser (September 9, 2009) quoted former Republican Senator Chuck Hagel on the enormous stakes involved in the *Citizens United* case:

> Chuck Hagel, the Nebraska Republican who retired from the Senate last year after serving two terms, said in an interview that if restrictions on corporate money were lifted, "the lobbyists and operators . . . would run wild." Reversing the law would magnify corporate power in society and "be an astounding blow against good government, responsible government," Hagel said. "We would debase the system, so we would get to the point where we couldn't govern ourselves."

Justice Louis Brandeis, one of the nation's greatest Supreme Court justices, once said, "The most important political office is that of the private citizen." Today's Supreme Court decision rejects Justice Brandeis's view, raising corporations to new heights of importance and influence in our political system.

The Supreme Court Was Correct Not to Restrict Political Speech

Glenn Greenwald

Glenn Greenwald is a US lawyer, an author, and a columnist and blogger at Salon.com, where he focuses on political and legal topics.

The Supreme Court yesterday [January 21, 2010], in a 5–4 decision, declared unconstitutional (on First Amendment grounds) campaign finance regulations which restrict the ability of corporations and unions to use funds from their general treasury for "electioneering" purposes. The case, *Citizens United v. [Federal Election Commission]*, presents some very difficult free speech questions, and I'm deeply ambivalent about the Court's ruling. There are several dubious aspects of the majority's opinion (principally its decision to invalidate the entire campaign finance scheme rather than exercising "judicial restraint" through a narrower holding). Beyond that, I believe that corporate influence over our political process is easily one of the top sicknesses afflicting our political culture. But there are also very real First Amendment interests implicated by laws which bar entities from spending money to express political viewpoints.

The Issue Is the First Amendment

I want to begin by examining several of the most common reactions among critics of this decision, none of which seems persuasive to me. Critics emphasize that the Court's ruling will produce very bad outcomes: primarily that it will severely

Glenn Greenwald, "What the Supreme Court Got Right," *Salon.com*, January 22, 2010. This article first appeared in Salon.com, at http://www.Salon.com. An online version remains in the Salon archives. Reprinted with permission.

exacerbate the problem of corporate influence in our democracy. Even if this is true, it's not really relevant. Either the First Amendment allows these speech restrictions or it doesn't. In general, a law that violates the Constitution can't be upheld because the law produces good outcomes (or because its invalidation would produce bad outcomes).

The reality is that our political institutions are already completely beholden to and controlled by large corporate interests.

One of the central lessons of the [George W.] Bush era should have been that illegal or unconstitutional actions— warrantless eavesdropping, torture, unilateral presidential programs—can't be justified because of the allegedly good results they produce (Protecting us from the Terrorists). The "rule of law" means we faithfully apply it in ways that produce outcomes we like and outcomes we don't like. Denouncing court rulings because they invalidate laws one likes is what the Right often does (see how they reflexively and immediately protest every state court ruling invaliding opposite-sex-only marriage laws without bothering to even read about the binding precedents), and that behavior is irrational in the extreme. If the Constitution or other laws bar the government action in question, then that's the end of the inquiry; whether those actions produce good results is really not germane. Thus, those who want to object to the Court's ruling need to do so on First Amendment grounds. Except to the extent that some constitutional rights give way to so-called "compelling state interests," that the Court's decision will produce "bad results" is not really an argument.

More specifically, it's often the case that banning certain kinds of speech would produce good outcomes, and conversely, allowing certain kinds of speech produces bad outcomes (that's true for, say, white supremacist or neo-Nazi speech, or speech advocating violence against civilians). The First Amendment is not and never has been outcome-dependent; the government is barred from restricting speech—especially political speech—no matter the good results that would result from the restrictions. That's the price we pay for having the liberty of free speech. And even on a utilitarian level, the long-term dangers of allowing the government to restrict political speech invariably outweigh whatever benefits accrue from such restrictions.

Corporate Money in Politics

I'm also quite skeptical of the apocalyptic claims about how this decision will radically transform and subvert our democracy by empowering corporate control over the political process. My skepticism is due to one principal fact: I really don't see how things can get much worse in that regard. The reality is that our political institutions are already completely beholden to and controlled by large corporate interests. . . . Corporations find endless ways to circumvent current restrictions—their armies of PACs [political action committees], lobbyists, media control, and revolving-door rewards flood Washington and currently ensure their stranglehold—and while this decision will make things marginally worse, I can't imagine how it could worsen fundamentally. All of the hand-wringing sounds to me like someone expressing serious worry that a new law in North Korea will make the country more tyrannical. There's not much room for our corporatist political system to get more corporatist. Does anyone believe that the ability of corporations to influence our political process was meaningfully limited before yesterday's issuance of this ruling?

I'm even more un-persuaded by the argument—seen in today's *New York Times* Editorial—that this decision will "ensure that Republican candidates will be at an enormous advantage in future elections." What evidence is there for that? Over the past five years, corporate money has poured far more into the coffers of the Democratic Party than the GOP [Grand Old Party, nickname for the Republican Party]—and far more into [Barack] Obama's campaign coffers than [John] McCain's (especially from Wall Street). If anything, unlimited corporate money will be far more likely to strengthen incumbents than either of the two parties (and unlimited union spending, though dwarfed by corporate spending, will obviously benefit Democrats more). Besides, if it were the case that this law restricts the ability of Republicans far more than Democrats to raise money in election cycles, doesn't that rather obviously intensify the First Amendment concerns?

Ignoring Precedent

Then there's the always intellectually confused discussions of *stare decisis* [a legal principle requiring judges to respect earlier case law] and precedent. It's absolutely true that the *Citizens United* majority cavalierly tossed aside decades of judicial opinions upholding the constitutionality of campaign finance restrictions. But what does that prove? Several of the liberals' most cherished Supreme Court decisions did the same (*Brown v. Board of Education [of Topeka]* rejected *Plessy v. Ferguson*; *Lawrence v. Texas* overruled *Bowers v. Hardwick*, etc.). Beyond that, the central principle which critics of this ruling find most offensive—that corporations possess "personhood" and are thus entitled to constitutional (and First Amendment) rights—has also been affirmed by decades of Supreme Court jurisprudence; tossing that principle aside would require deviating from *stare decisis* every bit as much as the majority did here. If a settled proposition of law is sufficiently repugnant to the Constitution, then the Court is not only permitted, but required, to uproot it.

Ultimately, I think the free speech rights burdened by campaign finance laws are often significantly understated. I understand and sympathize with the argument that corporations are creatures of the state and should not enjoy the same rights as individuals. And one can't help but note the vile irony that Muslim "War on Terror" detainees have been essentially declared by some courts not to be "persons" under the Constitution, whereas corporations are.

But the speech restrictions struck down by *Citizens United* do not only apply to Exxon and Halliburton; they also apply to nonprofit advocacy corporations, such as, say, the ACLU [American Civil Liberties Union] and Planned Parenthood, as well as labor unions, which are genuinely burdened in their ability to express their views by these laws. I tend to take a more absolutist view of the First Amendment than many people, but laws which prohibit organized groups of people— which is what corporations are—from expressing political views goes right to the heart of free speech guarantees no matter how the First Amendment is understood. Does anyone doubt that the facts that gave rise to this case—namely, the government's banning the release of a critical film about Hillary Clinton by Citizens United—is exactly what the First Amendment was designed to avoid? And does anyone doubt that the First Amendment bars the government from restricting the speech of organizations composed of like-minded citizens who band together in corporate form to work for a particular cause?

What is overlooked in virtually every discussion I've seen over the last 24 hours is how ineffective these campaign finance laws are. Large corporations employ teams of lawyers and lobbyists and easily circumvent these restrictions; wealthy individuals and well-funded unincorporated organizations are unlimited in what they can spend. It's the smaller nonprofit advocacy groups whose political speech tends to be most burdened by these laws. Campaign finance laws are a bit like gun control statutes: actual criminals continue to possess large stockpiles of weapons, but law-abiding citizens are disarmed.

In sum, there's no question that the stranglehold corporations exert on our democracy is one of the most serious and pressing threats we face. I've written volumes on that very problem. Although I doubt it, this decision may very well worsen that problem in some substantial way. But on both pragmatic and constitutional grounds, the issue of corporate influence—like virtually all issues—is not really solvable by restrictions on political speech. Isn't it far more promising to have the government try to equalize the playing field through serious public financing of campaigns than to try to slink around the First Amendment—or, worse, amend it—in order to limit political advocacy?

There are few features that are still extremely healthy and vibrant in the American political system; the First Amendment is one of them, and the last thing we should want is Congress trying to limit it through amendments or otherwise circumvent it in the name of elevating our elections. Meaningful public financing of campaigns would far more effectively achieve the ostensible objectives of campaign finance restrictions without any of the dangers or constitutional infirmities. If yesterday's decision provides the impetus for that to be done, then it will have, on balance, achieved a very positive outcome, even though that was plainly not its intent.

Corporate Campaign Spending Gives Corporations Little Influence over Government

Sheldon Richman

Sheldon Richman is editor of the Freeman: Ideas on Liberty, *a publication of the Foundation for Economic Education, a free-market organization founded to advance the freedom philosophy.*

It's funny how the people who push hardest for government intervention in more and more areas are the first to gripe that everything has become politicized. What were they expecting? Did they forget that government is a political institution?

Money and Politics

Paul Krugman and Chris Matthews, among other Progressives, are apoplectic because two senators of the minority party held up votes on [President Barack] Obama appointments in order to win pork-barrel projects for their states. This reminds me of Captain Renault's [a fictional movie character] reaction to learning that people gamble in Rick's gin joint.

Krugman acknowledges that this sort of thing is old hat, but he is upset that it's become more common. Perhaps, but it was only a matter of time before the device known as the "hold" would be more widely used. The stakes have gotten higher over the years.

How in the world could the central government commandeer $3.8 trillion—about a third of it borrowed—without reelection-hungry politicians being willing to walk over their mothers to get at that honey pot?

Sheldon Richman, "Corruption in Government? Shocking! The Circle Can't Be Squared," TheFreemanOnline.org, February 12 2010. © 2010 by Foundation for Economic Education. Reproduced by permission.

When someone insists he can square the circle, you know you're looking at a demagogue or a zealot. Same goes for someone who insists you can have a government that exercises plenary powers over our lives without generating *politics* in the most unsavory sense of the word. I suspect that people like Krugman and Matthews know you can't have one without the other, but they would like to have it so bad that they feign shock when a senator holds up a vote until he gets a government contract and some superfluous building for his state.

It's hard to show statistically that money has a large and systematic influence on political outcomes.

People of this ilk showed the same reaction when the Supreme Court ruled recently that corporations (for- and nonprofit) and unions cannot be barred from spending political money during election campaigns. (McCain-Feingold [a 2002 campaign finance law, also known as the Bipartisan Campaign Reform Act] outlawed so-called independent expenditures by all incorporated entities, except media companies, 30 days before a primary and 60 days before a general election. The Court said that is unconstitutional.) Progressives are appalled that such entities would try to influence the selection of officeholders in a government that holds life-and-death power over so many aspects of life. Did they think people with interests at stake would just stand by passively? Apparently so, and when the affected organizations refused to stand by, the "good-government" crowd opted for gagging them, showing unmistakably how devoted that crowd is to free speech when the chips are down. Now they (and Obama) blast the five Supreme Court justices for saying the gag is unconstitutional.

One need not love big corporations or big unions—both of which derive significant power from the State—to be offended by this restriction on freedom of speech. Remember the slippery slope! Whose speech might next be deemed *too* influential and in need of restricting? Besides, it's not as though corporations and unions have no other ways to influence politicians and policies. I suspect that spending during campaigns is the weakest method of influencing the government. Voters still have to go into the booth and mark the "right" ballots, and politicians can't risk alienating the median voter. As [economist] Tyler Cowen points out:

> For all the anecdotal evidence, it's hard to show statistically that money has a large and systematic influence on political outcomes. That is partly because politicians cannot stray too far from public opinion. (In part, it is also because interest groups get their way on many issues by supplying an understaffed Congress with ideas and intellectual resources, not by running ads or making donations.) It is quite possible that the Court's decision won't affect election results very much.

So, memo to Krugman, Matthews, et al.: You can't have the kind of government you want *without* people inside and outside the halls going to great lengths to get their hands on that power. You know it, and so does anyone who spends five minutes thinking it through. Enough whining already.

The Need to Shrink Government

Of course, what I just said suggests the way to end the power brokering, logrolling, and influence peddling:

Don't let government commandeer our resources and manage our lives!

If there are no privileges to sell, there are no privileges to buy.

I'm sure the Progressives are saying, "Gosh, why didn't we think of that?"

Well, no, not really. They apparently would sacrifice anything to preserve the machinery of social engineering, which they need to realize their grand designs. They rhapsodize about democracy, but their words betray their true preferences. Why else would they insist that Obamacare [Obama's plan for health care reform] be passed despite the opposition of a majority of the public? Why do they smugly insist that the only reason the people are against it is that Obama did not explain the 2,500-page plan clearly enough in dozens of speeches?

When will the Progressives realize that although they claim to despise corporate influence in government, it is their Progressive forebears who helped forge the implements of power to which the corporate world has ready access.

This government doesn't merely *breed* corruption. It *is* corruption.

The *Citizens United* Decision Involved Issues of Speech, Not Contributions to Candidates

John Samples

John Samples is director of the Cato Institute's Center for Representative Government.

Many people say the Supreme Court's decision in *Citizens United [v. Federal Election Commission]* is harming American democracy. Is it? Everyone knows democracy means "government by the people." But what does that mean concretely?

Enforcing the Constitution

The people should select those who govern. Each citizen should have an equal vote on who holds office. But it involves more than voting. Citizens need information to judge candidates. There is no shortage of people willing to inform voters if government respects freedom of speech, of the press, and of association. The First Amendment guarantees these freedoms. It is a vital part of democracy.

Until last January, Congress prohibited corporations (including labor unions and some advocacy groups) from funding speech advocating the election or defeat of a candidate for federal office. In *Citizens United*, the Supreme Court voided this ban on First Amendment grounds. These organizations may now spend freely on political speech.

Citizens United has critics. Incumbents fear new speakers will lead to electoral defeats. Other critics believe the First Amendment applies only to "natural" persons and not to legal individuals like corporations.

John Samples, "The First Amendment Guarantees the *Citizens United* Decision," *US News & World Report*, September 27, 2010. USNews.com. Reproduced by permission.

The Constitution says otherwise. The Constitution indicates when a right or opportunity is limited to citizens or persons. The 15th Amendment protects the right "of citizens" to vote and defends against racial discrimination. The privileges and immunities of citizens are protected elsewhere as well. Only citizens are eligible for the presidency. The Constitution also mentions "persons" in several places. The First Amendment says only that Congress "shall make no law . . . abridging the freedom of speech." It does not say "the freedom of speech of citizens." The speech, not the speaker, is important, and it cannot be denied that Congress prohibited speech prior to *Citizens United*.

Citizens United *did not involve contributions to candidates or parties. The money at issue funds speech, not candidates. The question of corruption is not relevant.*

Equality of Speech

Others say businesses will dominate debate. Democracy, they assert, means everyone should have an equal say during elections. We do not know the future, but we have some evidence from the past. In 2002, when corporations and labor unions could contribute soft money to the parties, such donations were evenly split.

There is a deeper question here. Does maintaining equal voice in a democracy justify limiting the speech of those who say "too much"? The Supreme Court in 1976 said such rationales for restricting speech were "wholly foreign to the First Amendment." Why? To attain equality of speech, government would have to limit those who spoke too much. Equal speech could not be free. The media and its freedom of the press would not be exempt from these limits. *The New York Times* and *Fox News* enjoy more speech than average Americans.

Fortunately for media corporations, Citizens United recognized that our Constitution favors freedom over equality of speech.

Critics argue that newly freed corporate spending will corrupt the legislature by buying favors for the few at a cost to most voters. Courts have allowed Congress to regulate contributions to prevent such corruption. But *Citizens United* did not involve contributions to candidates or parties. The money at issue funds speech, not candidates. The question of corruption is not relevant.

Government by the people requires an equal vote and the freedom to speak and associate. Democracy also requires toleration of unpopular speech. When government and citizens fall short of those ideals, the courts should act. In *Citizens United*, the Supreme Court fulfilled that obligation.

CHAPTER 4

What Are the Remedies for US Government Corruption?

Chapter Preface

One solution that has been proposed to counter the influence of private money in US politics is publicly financed elections. This idea was first proposed in the early twentieth century, when Progressive Era reformers battled the political influence wielded by wealthy industrial barons. In his 1907 State of the Union address, President Theodore Roosevelt proposed public funding of federal elections and a ban on private contributions. The president succeeded in passing the Tillman Act of 1907, which banned corporate contributions to all political campaigns, but his public financing proposal was not enacted. Decades later, in 1966, the US Congress passed a bill providing for public funding of presidential elections, but the law was suspended a year later.

The idea of public presidential financing finally became law, however, in 1971. That year, the Revenue Act provided for presidential nominees in general elections to receive public monies from a Presidential Election Campaign Fund in the US Treasury, created by allowing taxpayers a voluntary check-off option in their federal income tax returns. Using these funds, the federal government matches up to $250 of each individual's contribution to the candidate. Candidates who choose to receive public funding, however, must agree to limit campaign spending to certain amounts. This system of public financing of presidential campaigns was completed with the passage of the 1971 Federal Election Campaign Act, which extended the public financing provisions of the Revenue Act to presidential primary elections and the nominating conventions of national political parties. The Presidential Election Campaign Fund is still in effect today, allowing presidential candidates to opt for public financing and opt out of private fund-raising. The goal of this program is both to liberate candidates from having to raise large campaign contributions and to reduce the cost of running for office.

The current federal public funding law, however, only applies to presidential elections. Also, although presidential candidates routinely opted for public financing in the 1970s and 1980s, in recent years a number of serious presidential candidates have opted out of public financing because they feel they can raise more money from private sources. During the 2000 Republican primary campaign, for example, then-presidential candidate George W. Bush opted out of receiving presidential public financing largely because another Republican candidate, wealthy businessman Steve Forbes, opted to use his own monies to support his candidacy. In 2004, Bush again opted out of the system during the primary campaign, instead financing his reelection campaign with over $200 million in private donations, far more than the $44 million spending limit for publicly financed candidates. And since Bush opted out during the primaries, Democratic presidential candidates Howard Dean and John Kerry also chose not to receive public funds in the primary election. And in the 2008 presidential election, Democratic presidential candidate Barack Obama became the first presidential candidate to opt out of public funding for the general presidential election; instead, Obama waged a successful Internet fund-raising campaign, collecting over $200 million, much of it in small donations—far more than the $84.1 million limit that he would have faced as a publicly funded candidate.

In the late 1990s, a grassroots movement emerged to create public funding for congressional and local elections. This movement, called Clean Elections (or Clean Money), has succeeded in passing public financing laws in eight states and two municipalities—Maine (1996), Vermont (1997), Arizona (1998), Massachusetts, North Carolina (2002), New Mexico (2003), New Jersey (2004), and Connecticut as well as Portland, Oregon (2005) and Albuquerque, New Mexico (2005). Clean Elections remains the law in all these places with the exception of Massachusetts.

Many who criticize the undue influence of corporations in politics would like to expand federal law to provide for federal funding of all congressional elections. In March 2007, bills containing this concept were introduced in the US Congress— the Fair Elections Now Act in the Senate and the Clean Money, Clean Elections Act in the House. The Fair Elections Now Act was reintroduced in both houses of Congress in both 2009 and 2010 but has yet to be enacted. If ultimately passed, the law would give all federal congressional candidates the option to qualify for public funding to run their campaigns. Even if passed, however, some commentators question whether the current US Supreme Court, which has issued rulings striking down campaign finance laws, might overturn or undermine a public financing scheme.

The authors of the viewpoints in this chapter discuss the Fair Elections Now Act as well as other ideas aimed at rooting out government corruption.

More Extensive Financial Reform Will Be Needed to Fix Wall Street

Rob Weissman

Rob Weissman is the president of Public Citizen, an organization that works to ensure that all citizens are represented in Congress.

More than a year and a half after Wall Street crashed the global economy, Congress has finally taken important action to rein in the Wall Street titans. The Wall Street reform bill [Dodd-Frank Wall Street Reform and Consumer Protection Act] is a crucial first step, passed despite the financial sector's enormous investments in lobbying and campaign contributions. But Wall Street remains far too powerful in Washington, with the result that this bill does not contain crucial reforms that must be included in subsequent reform efforts.

On the positive side of the ledger, the bill contains stronger consumer financial protections and curbs on some of the worst practices in the derivatives markets.

Consumer Protection

The bill consolidates and streamlines existing consumer financial protection by creating a Consumer Financial Protection Bureau. This bureau will have the authority to crack down on unfair, deceptive and abusive practices in connection with consumer products such as payday loans, credit cards and mortgages by using new rules and enforcement powers. It also will have authority to ban particularly harmful practices such as forced arbitration. Had the bureau been in place and operating effectively during the run-up to the financial crisis it

Rob Weissman, "Congress Passes Financial Reform; Much More Must Be Done to Rein in Wall Street," *Public Citizen*, July 15, 2010. Pubcit.typepad.com. Reproduced by permission.

would have prevented the predatory and abusive mortgage lending practices that led directly to the crash.

Transparency, Oversight and Stability in the Over-the-Counter Derivatives Market

The bill also makes major progress on reining in reckless and unfair derivatives practices. It restricts the most egregious practices, such as federally insured banks engaging in risky proprietary trading and financial institutions making bets against their own clients. It requires the vast majority of previously unregulated OTC [over-the-counter] derivatives to be cleared and traded on regulated exchanges. Derivatives were a critical cause of the financial crisis; new clearing and exchange rules should go a long way toward stabilizing the system.

There are many other positive components of the bill. How effective they turn out to be will depend crucially on implementation over the next months and years. If Wall Street can regain control of the regulatory process, then many of the potential benefits from this bill will be lost.

Particularly because it does not break up the megabanks, this bill does not ensure that we will not have a repeat of the financial crisis.

Missing Elements

Unfortunately, many important reforms are missing from the bill. Some key elements were jettisoned or weakened in the conference process. These include limits on commercial banks owning hedge funds, and the bulk of the requirement that commercial banks spin off their derivatives trading desks.

Other key reforms are absent from the bill. These include meaningful restraints on executive and top trader compensation, a financial speculation tax and rules to break up the biggest banks. The megabanks that now dominate the financial sector—which is more concentrated than at the onset of the financial crisis—pose a continuing threat to our economy and democracy.

Particularly because it does not break up the megabanks, this bill does not ensure that we will not have a repeat of the financial crisis. Another round of reform will be needed to achieve that objective. Nonetheless, the bill is an extraordinary achievement for regular Americans and will be enacted into law despite a massive and deceptive opposition campaign by Wall Street and its allies.

We have lots more to do, but today we have achieved what many thought impossible just months ago.

The Financial Crisis Creates an Opportunity for Fundamental Economic Reform

David Korten

David Korten is cofounder and board chair of YES!, *an online magazine dedicated to encouraging visionary solutions to the world's biggest problems.*

Whether it was divine providence or just good luck, we should give thanks that financial collapse hit us before the worst of global warming and peak oil. As challenging as the economic meltdown may be, it buys time to build a new economy that serves life rather than money. It lays bare the fact that the existing financial system has brought our way of life and the natural systems on which we depend to the brink of collapse. This wake-up call is inspiring unprecedented numbers of people to take action to bring forth the culture and institutions of a new economy that can serve us and sustain our living planet for generations into the future.

The world of financial stability, environmental sustainability, economic justice, and peace that most psychologically healthy people want is possible if we replace a defective operating system that values only money, seeks to monetize every relationship, and pits each person in a competition with every other for dominance.

From Economic Power to Basket Case

Not long ago, the news was filled with stories of how Wall Street's money masters had discovered the secrets of creating limitless wealth through exotic financial maneuvers that elimi-

David Korten, "Why This Crisis May Be Our Best Chance to Build a New Economy," YesMagazine.org, June 19, 2009. Reproduced by permission.

nated both risk and the burden of producing anything of real value. In an audacious social engineering experiment, corporate interests drove a public policy shift that made finance the leading sector of the U.S. economy and the concentration of private wealth the leading economic priority.

Corporate interests drove a policy agenda that rolled back taxes on high incomes, gave tax preference to income from financial speculation over income from productive work, cut back social safety nets, drove down wages, privatized public assets, outsourced jobs and manufacturing capacity, and allowed public infrastructure to deteriorate. They envisioned a world in which the United States would dominate the global economy by specializing in the creation of money and the marketing and consumption of goods produced by others.

As a result, manufacturing fell from 27 percent of U.S. gross domestic product in 1950 to 12 percent in 2005, while financial services grew from 11 percent to 20 percent. From 1980 to 2005, the highest-earning 1 percent of the U.S. population increased its share of taxable income from 9 percent to 19 percent, with most of the gain going to the top one-tenth of 1 percent. The country became a net importer, with a persistent annual trade deficit of more than three-quarters of a trillion dollars financed by rising foreign debt. Wall Street insiders congratulated themselves on their financial genius even as they turned the United States into a national economic basket case and set the stage for global financial collapse.

All the reports of financial genius masked the fact that a phantom-wealth economy is unsustainable. Illusory assets based on financial bubbles, abuse of the power of banks to create credit (money) from nothing, corporate asset stripping, baseless credit ratings, and creative accounting led to financial, social, and environmental breakdown. The system suppressed the wages of the majority while continuously cajoling them to buy more than they could afford using debt that they had no means to repay.

A Defective Operating System

The operating system of our phantom-wealth economy was written by and for Wall Street interests for the sole purpose of making more money for people who have money. It makes cheap money readily available to speculators engaged in inflating financial bubbles and financing other predatory money scams. It makes money limited and expensive to those engaged in producing real wealth—life, and the things that sustain life—and pushes the productive members of society into indebtedness to those who produce nothing at all.

In the world we want, the organization of economic life mimics healthy ecosystems that are locally rooted, highly adaptive, and self-reliant in food and energy.

Money, the ultimate object of worship among modern humans, is the most mysterious of human artifacts: a magic number with no meaning or existence outside the human mind. Yet it has become the ultimate arbiter of life—deciding who will live in grand opulence in the midst of scarcity and who will die of hunger in the midst of plenty.

The monetization of relationships—replacing mutual caring with money as the primary medium of exchange—accelerated after World War II when growth in Gross National Product, essentially growth in monetized relationships, became the standard for evaluating economic performance. The work of the mother who cares for her child solely out of love counts for nothing. By contrast, the mother who leaves her child unattended to accept pay for tending the child of her neighbor suddenly becomes "economically productive." The result is a public policy bias in favor of monetizing relationships to create phantom wealth—money—at the expense of real wealth.

In the world we want, the organization of economic life mimics healthy ecosystems that are locally rooted, highly adaptive, and self-reliant in food and energy. Information and technology are shared freely, and trade between neighbors is fair and balanced.

We must reboot the economy with a new, values-based operating system designed to support social and environmental balance and the creation of real, living wealth.

In a modern economy, nearly every relationship essential to life depends on money. This gives ultimate power to those who control the creation and allocation of money. Five features of the existing money system virtually assure abuse.

1. Money issuance and allocation are controlled by private banks managed for the exclusive benefit of their top managers and largest shareholders.

2. Money issued by private banks as debt must be repaid with interest. This requires perpetual economic growth to create sufficient demand for new loans to create the money required to pay the interest due on previous loans. The fact that nearly every dollar in circulation is generating interest for bankers and their investors virtually assures an ever-increasing concentration of wealth.

3. The power to determine how much money will circulate and where it will flow is concentrated and centralized in a tightly interlinked system of private-benefit corporations that operate in secret, beyond public scrutiny, with the connivance of the Federal Reserve.

4. The Federal Reserve presents itself as a public institution responsible for exercising oversight, but it is accountable only to itself, operates primarily for the benefit of the largest Wall Street banks, and consistently favors the interests of those who live by returns to money over those who live by returns to their labor.

5. The lack of proper regulatory oversight allows players at each level of the system to make highly risky decisions, collect generous fees based on phantom profits, and pass the risk to others.

A Values-Based Operating System

To get ourselves out of our current mess and create the world we want, we must reboot the economy with a new, values-based operating system designed to support social and environmental balance and the creation of real, living wealth. We have seen what happens when government and big business operate in secret. The new system must be open to public scrutiny and democratic control. Globalization and the harshest form of capitalism have eroded the bonds of community and created vast gaps in wealth between the richest and the poorest. The new system must be locally rooted in strong communities and distribute wealth equitably.

Our environment and our infrastructure have paid a terrible price for the belief that private interests must always win over public ones. A viable system must balance public and private interests. Unregulated speculation is at the root of the current crisis. Society is better served by a system that favors productive work and investment, limits speculation, and suppresses inflation in all forms—including financial bubbles.

The following are five essential areas of action.

1. *Government-Issued Money.* There is urgent need for government action to create living wage jobs, rebuild public infrastructure, and restore domestic productive capacity. It is folly, however, for government to finance those projects by borrowing money created by the same private banks that created the financial mess.

The government can and should instead issue debt-free money to finance the stimulus and meet other public needs. Properly administered, this money will flow to community-based enterprises and help revitalize Main Street market economies engaged in the production of real wealth.

2. *Community Banking.* Under the bailout, the government is buying ownership shares in failed Wall Street banks with the expectation of eventually reselling them to private interests. So far, the money has disappeared or gone to acquisitions, management bonuses, office remodeling, and fancy vacations with no noticeable effect on the freeing up of credit.

A better plan, as many economists are recommending, is to force bankrupt banks into government receivership. As part of the sale and distribution of assets to meet creditor claims, these banks should be broken up and their local branches sold to local investors. These new, individual community banks and mutual savings and loan associations should be chartered to serve Main Street needs, lending to local manufacturers, merchants, farmers, and homeowners within a strong regulatory framework.

3. *Real-Wealth Investment.* Gambling should be confined to licensed casinos. Contrary to the claims of Wall Street, financial speculation does not create real wealth, serves no public interest, and should be strongly discouraged. Tax the purchase or sale of financial instruments and impose a tax surcharge on short-term capital gains. Make it illegal to sell, insure, or borrow against an asset you do not own, or to issue a financial security not backed by a real asset. This would effectively shut down much of Wall Street, which would be a positive result.

The money that has been used for speculation must be redirected to productive investment that creates real wealth and meets our essential needs responsibly, equitably, and sustainably using green technologies and closed-loop production cycles. We can begin by eliminating subsidies for carbon fuels and putting a price on greenhouse gas emissions. We can revise trade agreements to affirm the responsibility of every nation to contribute to global economic security and stability by organizing for sustainable self-reliance in food and energy and managing its economy to keep imports and exports in balance. If we Americans learn to live within our means, we will free up resources others need to feed, clothe, and house themselves and their families. The notion that reducing our consumption would harm others is an example of the distorted logic of a phantom-wealth economy.

4. *Middle Class Fiscal Policy*. The ruling financial elites have used their control of fiscal policy to conduct a class war that has decimated the once celebrated American middle class and led to economic disaster. Markets work best when economic power is equitably distributed and individuals contribute to the economy as both workers and owners. Massive inequality in income and ownership assures the failure of both markets and democracy.

To restore the social fabric and allocate real resources in ways that serve the needs of all, we must restore the middle class through equity-oriented fiscal policies. There is also a strong moral argument that those who profited from creating our present economic mess should bear the major share of the cost of cleaning it up. It is time to reinstitute the policies that created the American middle class after World War II. Restore progressive income tax with a top rate of 90 percent and favor universal participation in responsible ownership and a family wage. Because no one has a natural birth entitlement to any greater share of the real wealth of society than anyone else, use the estate tax to restore social balance at the end of each lifetime in a modern equivalent of the Biblical Jubilee, which called for periodically forgiving debts and restoring land to its original owners.

5. *Responsible Enterprise*. Enterprises in a market economy need a fair return to survive. This imposes a necessary discipline. Service to the community, however, rather than profit, is the primary justification for the firm's existence. As Wall

Street has so graphically demonstrated, profit is not a reliable measure of social contribution.

Enterprises are most likely to serve their communities when they are human-scale and owned by responsible local investors with an active interest in their operation beyond mere profit. Concentrations of corporate power reduce public accountability, and no corporation should be too big to fail. The new economy will use antitrust to break large corporations into their component parts and sell them to responsible local owners. There are many ways to aggregate economic resources that do not create concentrations of monopoly power or encourage absentee ownership. These include the many forms of worker, cooperative, and community ownership and cooperative alliances among locally rooted firms.

Current proposals for dealing with the economic collapse fall far short of dealing with the deep conflict of values and interests at the core of the current economic crisis. We face an urgent need to expand and deepen the debate to advance options that go far beyond anything currently on the table.

The World We Want

The world of our shared human dream is one where people live happy, productive lives in balance with one another and Earth. It is democratic and middle class without extremes of wealth or poverty. It is characterized by strong, stable families and communities in which relationships are defined primarily by mutual trust and caring. Every able adult is both a worker and an owner. Most families own their own home and have an ownership stake in their local economy. Everyone has productive work and is respected for his or her contribution to the well-being of the community.

In the world we want, the organization of economic life mimics healthy ecosystems that are locally rooted, highly adaptive, and self-reliant in food and energy. Information and technology are shared freely, and trade between neighbors is fair and balanced. Each community, region and nation strives to live within its own means in balance with its own environmental resources. Conflicts are resolved peacefully and no group seeks to expropriate the resources of its neighbors. Competition is for excellence, not domination.

The financial collapse has revealed the extreme corruption of the Wall Street financial system and created an extraordinary opening for change. We cannot, however, expect the leadership to come from within the political system. There is good reason why both the [George W.] Bush and [Barack] Obama administrations, different as they are, have responded to the Wall Street crash with bailouts for the guilty rather than face up to the need for a radical restructuring of the financial system. No president can stand up against Wall Street absent massive popular demand.

To move forward, we the people must build a powerful popular political movement demanding a new economy designed to serve our children, families, communities, and nature. It begins with a conversation to demystify money and expose the lie that there is no alternative to the present economic system. It continues with action to rebuild our local economies based on sound market principles backed by national political action to transform the money system and broaden participation in ownership. This is our moment of opportunity.

The DISCLOSE Act Provides Transparency for Corporate Political Advertising

Chris Van Hollen and Mike Castle

Chris Van Hollen is a Democratic representative from Maryland. Mike Castle is a Republican representative from Delaware.

Editor's Note: As of November 2010, the DISCLOSE [Democracy Is Strengthened by Casting Light on Spending in Elections] Act had passed the House but failed to pass in the Senate.

On Jan. 21, 2010, the Supreme Court threw out 100 years of established law and legal precedent that protected the integrity of our political process against direct campaign expenditures by big-money special interests. With Americans already struggling to have their voices heard in Washington, the ruling in *Citizens United v. Federal Election Commission* dramatically expanded the ability of special interests to influence the political process.

The DISCLOSE Act Promotes Transparency

The most important things Congress can do in response to this ruling are to increase transparency and shine a light on the special interests trying to influence elections. That is why we have introduced the bipartisan DISCLOSE (Democracy Is Strengthened by Casting Light on Spending in Elections) Act. The bill requires the disclosure of political spending by special interests, keeps foreign-controlled companies from affecting America's elections, and ensures that entities that receive large amounts of taxpayer money can't turn around and spend that

Chris Van Hollen and Mike Castle, "The Disclose Act Is a Matter of Campaign Honesty," *The Washington Post*, June 17, 2010. WashingtonPost.com. Reproduced by permission.

money in campaigns. By bringing campaign spending into the light, we empower voters to make more informed decisions.

The DISCLOSE Act ensures that Americans will know when a company or labor union is seeking to influence campaigns. It prevents special interests from hiding behind third-party groups, sham organizations and dummy corporations by requiring the heads of organizations to "stand by their ad" the same way political candidates must take personal responsibility for their ads. Moreover, the bill mandates that an organization seeking to influence an election list the top five contributors onscreen at the end of its ad.

American elections should be decided by Americans, not foreign corporations. Under the DISCLOSE Act, U.S. corporations that are controlled by foreign interests and foreign companies—such as BP and those owned by hostile foreign governments—would be barred from making political expenditures in U.S. elections. Right now, Citgo—a wholly owned subsidiary of the Venezuelan government—could spend freely in American elections with minimal difficulty if the Court's ruling is not addressed.

Finally, the DISCLOSE Act prohibits organizations that receive large amounts of taxpayer money from using those funds to try to influence elections. Wall Street banks, for example, would not be allowed to take government money and recycle it in efforts to defeat lawmakers who are fighting to rein in the banks' irresponsible behavior. The last thing we need in this time of soaring deficits is for taxpayer money to be used to try to buy elections.

Citizen Organizations Support the DISCLOSE Act

Some have raised concerns about proposals that allow a narrow exemption for certain reporting requirements for large, long-standing citizen-based organizations on the condition that they spend no corporate donations for campaign purposes. While we prefer our original bill, with equal treatment of all organizations, this legislation will still shine an unprecedented amount of sunlight on campaign expenditures. That is why Common Cause, Public Citizen, Democracy 21, the Campaign Legal Center and the League of Women Voters strongly support this bill.

Overwhelmingly, Americans support tougher campaign finance laws, polls show, including efforts to undo the damage done by *Citizens United*. The people recognize that this decision, if left unchecked, will allow shadowy special interests to engage in the buying and selling of elections.

Our legislation was crafted with input from Republicans, Democrats and a wide array of outside organizations. To date, the Senate bill has 47 cosponsors and the House bill has 114.

Opponents of reform and transparency cannot argue against the merits of this bipartisan legislation, which simply places disclosure requirements on political activities. As [Supreme Court] Justice Louis Brandeis said, "Sunlight is the best disinfectant." Ultimately, the DISCLOSE Act gives the American people the power of information and protects our democracy from being bought and sold by special interests.

The DISCLOSE Act Infringes on Corporate Free Speech

Tom Donohue

Tom Donohue is president and chief executive officer of the US Chamber of Commerce, a business federation representing companies, business associations, and state and local chambers in the United States.

Editor's Note: As of November 2010, the DISCLOSE [Democracy Is Strengthened by Casting Light on Spending in Elections] Act had passed the House but failed to pass in the Senate.

Though it comes wrapped in the language of transparency, the DISCLOSE Act has a far plainer intent—to discourage people from exercising their constitutional right to free speech. Introduced by two members of Congress tasked with winning elections—Rep. Chris Van Hollen (D-MD), the chairman of the Democratic Congressional Campaign Committee, and Sen. Chuck Schumer (D-NY), former chairman of the Democratic Senatorial Campaign Committee—this legislation threatens the First Amendment rights of businesses across the country.

Discriminatory Against Corporations

The bill's sponsors admit that its purpose is to deter corporations from participating in the political process. Sen. Schumer has said that the bill will make corporations "think twice" before attempting to influence election outcomes, and that this "deterrent effect should not be underestimated."

With an overwhelming—and unconstitutional—emphasis on limiting the speech of for-profit corporations and the asso-

Tom Donahue, "DISCLOSE Act Muzzles Business Free Enterprise," *U.S. Chamber Magazine*, June 2010. USChamberMagazine.com. Reproduced by permission.

ciations that represent them, the DISCLOSE Act discriminates against America's job creators, prohibiting them from expressing political views. The Schumer-Van Hollen bill, for example, places a blanket prohibition on all election-related speech by companies with federal contracts above a specific monetary threshold ($50,000 in the Senate; $7 million in the House). Of the thousands of businesses that regularly participate in contracts with the federal government, many would be categorically barred from making their political views known.

This prohibition on core political speech is directly inconsistent with a U.S. Supreme Court ruling that Congress can prohibit political speech only where it has evidence of quid pro quo corruption. There is no such evidence to support such a broad prohibition.

The bill's sponsors admit that its purpose is to deter corporations from participating in the political process.

Exempting Labor Unions

At the same time, the Schumer-Van Hollen bill effectively imposes no comparable restrictions on labor unions. Unions that receive federal grants, for instance, can continue to engage in political activities. This comes despite the fact that unions and their political action committees are the single largest contributors to political campaigns and claim to have spent nearly $450 million in the 2008 presidential race.

It's a sad day when legislators like Rep. Van Hollen and Sen. Schumer so blatantly put politics before the people's business. With unemployment near 10%, members of Congress should be more concerned about creating jobs than protecting their own. Stifling free speech is an abuse of the legislative process and is unconstitutional, and the U.S. Chamber of Commerce will not let this stand. Free speech does not corrupt our politics, but efforts to limit it do.

The Fair Elections Now Act Can Help Restore Public Confidence in Congress

Lawrence Lessig

Lawrence Lessig is a professor of law at Harvard Law School and cofounder of the nonprofit Change Congress, a nonpartisan advocacy organization that seeks to protect the independence of Congress by fighting the influence of money in politics.

The Supreme Court's decision in *Citizens United [v. Federal Election Commission]* has sparked a furious debate across the nation. At least a half a dozen organizations, and just as many members of Congress, are now pushing for a constitutional amendment to overturn it. Others are frantically trying to convince the nation that the speech of Exxon is as central to democracy as the protest of Rosa Parks.

The Problem of a Fund-Raising Congress

But in my view, the greatest danger of *Citizens United* is distraction. There are fundamental problems with America's democracy. An overly diverse speech market is not high on that list. And while the decision in *Citizens United*—if things stay as they are—could create a critical threat to American democracy, that is not because corporations get to speak. The danger in this decision is that it will further cement the corrupting dependency on private funding of public campaigns that already infects our Congress. The problem in our democracy is not diversity; the problem is a Congress dependent upon the fund-raisers. The problem is not corporate speech. The problem is the fund-raising Congress.

Lawrence Lessig, "A Call for a Convention," *The Huffington Post*, February 4, 2010. HuffingtonPost.com. © 2010 by The Huffington Post/AOL, Inc. Reproduced by permission of the publisher and the author.

For let us not forget: On the day before the Supreme Court decided *Citizens United*, we already had a problem with democracy in America. Already most Americans recognized that the Framers' ideal of a Congress "dependent upon the People" had become a slogan, not a reality. Already we had seen the devastating consequences of a Congress that seemed to care more about how it raises campaign dollars than how it enacts policy sense. Already democracy had failed.

[The Fair Elections Now Act] would fundamentally change the economy of influence in Washington.

Our task then was the same as it is now: to fix this fundamental flaw. Reversing *Citizens United* alone won't do that. Instead, we must begin the long and difficult process to restore independence to American democracy. That won't happen by Internet petition alone. It will require a long and serious national debate which begins by expressing respect to all sides, and inviting all sides to participate.

The Fair Elections Now Act

Now many of us—and I'm the first on this list—believe we can begin this process with an obvious first step first: with Congress enacting the Fair Elections Now Act, now. That statute would fundamentally change the economy of influence in Washington. By giving members an option to rely upon small dollar contributions alone (maxed at $100 a citizen), we could at least create the possibility that Congress would be filled with members whose integrity no one could doubt. That's not a promise that Congress would get everything right. But it is the assurance that when they get things wrong, Americans won't have to believe they betrayed principle or the public will because of money.

Overturning *Citizens United*

But there is a real and fair question about whether this Congress could pass such fundamental reform. More importantly, the Supreme Court's recent eagerness to overthrow any campaign finance regulation means there's a real and fair question whether even this reform would survive constitutional review.

Both questions have rightly led many to the conclusion that we need to think about these questions in a more fundamental way—that even if we get the Fair Elections Now Act, we need to begin a process to reform our fundamental law to assure that that change, or any change, sticks.

Thus, a gaggle of well-meaning souls, including, most prominently, [the advocacy group] MoveOn.org, have begun the process of organizing to get Congress to propose a constitutional amendment to overturn *Citizens United*, believing apparently that this single fundamental change is necessary and sufficient.

I agree that the Constitution needs to be reformed, in the sense that its founding principles need to be strengthened. But pushing Congress to propose an amendment overturning *Citizens United* now is, in my view, both a substantive and procedural mistake.

The substantive point I've already sketched: Reversing *Citizens United* is not enough. We need a more fundamental change to secure to Congress the power to protect its own independence—meaning independence from special interests, and a dependence upon the people. Silencing corporations is neither necessary nor sufficient to that objective.

The procedural point is more fundamental, and comes in two parts: First, no one should distract Congress from the one good thing it could do right now—pass the Fair Elections Now Act. That would be a huge victory; it is a possible victory; and we are defeating the cause of reform if we do anything that jeopardizes that possible win.

And second, we all need to recognize that America is uncertain about how best to fix our government right now. From the Tea Party Right to the Progressive Left, there is agreement that something fundamental has gone wrong. But I believe that our frustrations share a common source—an exasperation with the broken state of our political system—even as we disagree passionately on what to do about it.

A Constitutional Convention

The solution to that disagreement is democracy. We should begin the long discussion about how best to reform our democracy, to restore its commitment to liberty and a republic, by beginning a process to amend the Constitution through the one path the Framers gave us that has not yet been taken—a convention.

For the Framers imagined a time when the government might be captured. And they created a mechanism to respond to that capture. If 2/3rds of the legislatures of the states demand it, Congress must call a convention. That convention then must meet and deliberate about amendments to the constitution. If it agrees, it then proposes amendments to the states. 3/4ths of the states must then ratify any amendment before [it] becomes law. Thus, 12 states of 50 have the power to veto any change, meaning no change could happen unless it appealed to a solid group of Red States and a solid group of Blue.

We are, today, beginning the process to call a convention. We have our own view about the amendment that our Constitution needs. . . . But this effort will require a wide range of organized citizens to push their states to enact the resolution calling for a convention.

President Barack Obama Should Follow FDR's Example and Oppose Corporate Interests

Johann Hari

Johann Hari is a British journalist and writer and a columnist for the Independent, *a British newspaper, and the* Huffington Post, *an online US newsmagazine.*

This week [January 21, 2010], a disaster hit the United States, and the after-shocks will be shaking and breaking global politics for years. It did not grab the same press attention as the fall of liberal Kennedy-licking Massachusetts to a pick-up truck Republican, or President [Barack] Obama's first State of the Union address, or the possible break-up of Brangelina [actors Brad Pitt and Angelina Jolie] and their United Nations of adopted infants. But it took the single biggest problem dragging American politics towards brutality and dysfunction—and made it much, much worse. Yet it also showed the only path that Obama can now take to salvage his presidency.

Institutionalizing Bribery

For more than a century, the US has slowly put some limits—too few, too feeble—on how much corporations can bribe, bully or intimidate politicians. On Tuesday [January 26, 2010] they were burned away in one whoosh. The Supreme Court ruled that corporations can suddenly run political adverts during an election campaign—and there is absolutely no limit on how many, or how much they can spend. So if you anger the investment bankers by supporting legislation to break up

Johann Hari, "This Corruption in Washington Is Smothering America's Future," *The Independent*, January 29, 2010. Independent.co.uk. Reproduced by permission.

the too-big-to-fail banks, you will smack into a wall of 24/7 ads exposing your every flaw. If you displease oil companies by supporting legislation to deal with global warming, you will now be hit by a tsunami of advertising saying you are opposed to jobs and the American Way. If you rile the defence contractors by opposing the gargantuan war budget, you will face a smear-campaign calling you Soft on Terror.

Representative Alan Grayson says: "It basically institutionalises and legalises bribery on the largest scale imaginable. Corporations will now be able to reward the politicians that play ball with them—and beat to death the politicians that don't. . . You won't even hear any more about the Senator from Kansas. It'll be the Senator from General Electric or the Senator from Microsoft."

The US political system now operates within a corporate cage. If you want to run for office, you have to take corporate cash—and so you have to serve corporate interests.

To understand the impact this will have, you need to grasp how smaller sums of corporate money have already hijacked American democracy. Let's look at a case that is simple and immediate and every American can see in front of them: health care. The United States is the only major industrialised democracy that doesn't guarantee health care for all its citizens. The result is that, according to a detailed study by Harvard University, some 45,000 Americans die needlessly every year. That's equivalent to 15 9/11s [referring to the death toll in the September 11, 2001, terrorist attack on the United States] every year, or two Haitian earthquakes every decade.

This isn't because the American people like it this way. Gallup has found in polls for a decade now that two-thirds believe the government should guarantee care for every American: they are as good and decent and concerned for each

167

other as any European. No: it is because private insurance companies make a fortune today out of a system that doesn't cover the profit-less poor, and can turn away the sickest people as "uninsurable". So they pay for politicians to keep the system broken. They fund the election campaigns of politicians on both sides of the aisle and employ an army of lobbyists, and for their part those politicians veto any system that doesn't serve their paymasters.

Look for example at Joe Lieberman, the former Democratic candidate for vice president. He has taken $448,066 in campaign contributions from private health care companies while his wife raked in $2m [million] as one of their chief lobbyists, and he has blocked any attempt in the Senate to break the stranglehold of the health insurance companies and broaden coverage.

Bizarrely, the Supreme Court has decided that corporations are "persons", so they have the "right" to speak during elections.

The US political system now operates within a corporate cage. If you want to run for office, you have to take corporate cash—and so you have to serve corporate interests. Corporations are often blatant in their corruption: it's not unusual for them to give to both competing candidates in a Senate race, to ensure all sides are indebted to them. It has reached the point that lobbyists now often write the country's laws. Not metaphorically; literally. The former Republican congressman Walter Jones spoke out in disgust in 2006 when he found that drug company lobbyists were actually authoring the words of the Medicare prescription bill, and puppet-politicians were simply nodding it through.

The Results of Corporate Dominance

But what happens if politicians are serving the short-term profit-hunger of corporations, and not the public interest? You only have to look at the shuttered shops outside your window for the answer. The banks were rapidly deregulated from the Eighties through the Nineties because their lobbyists paid politicians on all sides, and demanded their payback in the rolled-back rules and tossed-away laws. As Senator Dick Durbin says simply: "The banks own the Senate," so they had to obey.

It is this corruption that has prevented [President] Barack Obama from achieving anything substantial in his first year in office. How do you re-regulate the banks, if the Senate is owned by Wall Street? How do you launch a rapid transition away from oil and coal to wind and solar, if the fossil fuel industry owns Congress? How do you break with a grab-the-oil foreign policy if Big Oil provides the invitation that gets you into the party of American politics?

His attempt at health care reform is dying because he thought he could only get through the Senate a system that the giant health care corporations and drug companies pre-approved. So he promised to keep the ban on bringing cheap drugs down from Canada, he pledged not to bargain over prices, and he damped the idea of having a public option that would make sure ordinary Americans could actually afford it. The result was a Quasimodo health care proposal so feeble and misshapen that even the people of Massachusetts turned away in disgust.

Yet the corporations that caused this crisis are now being given yet more power. Bizarrely, the Supreme Court has decided that corporations are "persons", so they have the "right" to speak during elections. But corporations are not people. Should they have the right to bear arms, or to vote? It would make as much sense. They are a legal fiction, invented by the state—and they can be fairly regulated to stop them devouring their creator. This is the same Supreme Court that ruled that the detainees at Guantánomo Bay are not "persons" under the constitution deserving basic protections. A court that says a living breathing human is less of a "person" than Lockheed Martin has gone badly awry.

Two Paths for President Obama

Obama now faces two paths—the [Bill] Clinton road, or the FDR [Franklin Delano Roosevelt] highway. After he lost his health care battle, Clinton decided to serve the corporate interests totally. He is the one who carried out the biggest rollback of banking laws, and saw the largest explosion of inequality since the 1920s. Some of Obama's advisers are now nudging him down that path: the appalling anti-Keynesian pledge for a spending freeze on social programmes for the next three years to pay down the deficit is one of their triumphs.

But there is another way. Franklin Roosevelt began his presidency trying to appease corporate interests—but he faced huge uproar and disgust at home when it became clear this left ordinary Americans stranded. He switched course. He turned his anger on "the malefactors of great wealth" and bragged: "I welcome the hatred. . . of the economic royalists." He put in place tough regulations that prevented economic disaster and spiralling inequality for three generations.

There were rare flashes of what Franklin Delano Obama would look like in his reaction to the Supreme Court decision. He said: "It is a major victory for Big Oil, Wall Street banks, health insurance companies, and other powerful interests that marshal their power every day in Washington to drown out the voices of everyday Americans." But he has spent far more time coddling those interests than taking them on. The great pressure of strikes and protests put on FDR hasn't yet arisen from a public dissipated into hopelessness by an appalling media that convinces them they are powerless and should wait passively for a Messiah.

Very little positive change can happen in the US until they clear out the temple of American democracy. In the State of the Union, Obama spent one minute on this problem, and proposed restrictions on lobbyists—but that's only the tiniest of baby steps. He evaded the bigger issue. If Americans want a democratic system, they have to pay for it—and that means fair state funding for political candidates. Candidates are essential for the system to work: you may as well begrudge paying for the polling booths, or the lever you pull. At the same time, the Supreme Court needs to be confronted: when the Court tried to stymie the New Deal, FDR tried to pack it with justices on the side of the people. Obama needs to be pressured by Americans to be as radical in democratising the Land of the Fee.

None of the crises facing us all—from the global banking system to global warming—can be dealt with if a tiny number of super-rich corporations have a veto over every inch of progress. If Obama flunks this challenge, he may as well put the US government on e-Bay—and sell it to the highest bidder. How would we spot the difference?

It Is Unlikely That the Corruption of American Politics Can Be Reversed

Godfrey Hodgson

Godfrey Hodgson was director of the Reuters Foundation Programme at Oxford University and, before that, served as the Observer's *correspondent in the United States and as foreign editor of the* Independent, *both British newspapers.*

For many years now, many informed observers—journalists, academics, even practitioners with tender consciences— have agreed that American politics is being ruined by money: by the abundance of money from special interests sloshing around Washington, and by the avidity with which all too many politicians pursue it, first to ensure their re-election, then for themselves.

Such different judges as Elizabeth Drew, the liberal columnist, and Jeffrey Birnbaum, an experienced investigative reporter and broadcaster, have powerfully argued this case. Robert G. Kaiser, the recently retired number two at the *Washington Post*, supplies an impeccably researched account of how lobbying works in Washington in his book, *So Damn Much Money*—whose title quotes a remark from Bob Strauss, the ultimate insider's insider in Washington, lawyer-lobbyist, politico and former Democratic Party chairman.

Lessig's Proposals

Now Lawrence Lessig, a professor [at] the Harvard Law School and former colleague of President [Barack] Obama at the University of Chicago, has written a long and agonised article blaming the president's frustration on the corruption of

Godfrey Hodgson, "The American Political System: Ruin and Reform," Opendemocracy .net, February 11, 2010. Reproduced by permission.

American politics by money, and suggesting two devices that might clean up the stables. Lessig's article is worth reading in full, though some brief extracts give a flavour:

> "(A) year into the presidency of Barack Obama, it is already clear that this administration is an opportunity missed. Not because it is too conservative. Not because it is too liberal. But because it is too conventional. Obama has given up the rhetoric of his early campaign—a campaign that promised to 'challenge the broken system in Washington' and to 'fundamentally change the way Washington works.' Indeed, 'fundamental change' is no longer even a hint."

> "At the center of our government lies a bankrupt institution: Congress. Not financially bankrupt, at least not yet, but politically bankrupt."

> "As fund-raising becomes the focus of Congress—as the parties force members to raise money for other members, as they reward the best fund-raisers with lucrative committee assignments and leadership positions—the focus of congressional 'work' shifts. Like addicts constantly on the lookout for their next fix, members grow impatient with anything that doesn't promise the kick of a campaign contribution. The first job is meeting the fund-raising target. Everything else seems cheap . . . This dance has in turn changed the character of Washington."

> "This democracy no longer works. Its central player has been captured. Corrupted. Controlled by an economy of influence disconnected from the democracy. Congress has developed a dependency foreign to the Framers' design. Corporate campaign spending, now liberated by the Supreme Court, will only make that dependency worse. 'A dependence' not, as the Federalist Papers celebrated it, 'on the People' but a dependency upon interests that have conspired to produce a world in which policy gets sold . . . No one, Republican or Democratic, who doesn't currently depend upon this system should accept it."

"What would the reform the Congress needs be? At its core, a change that restores institutional integrity. A change that rekindles a reason for America to believe in the central institution of its democracy by removing the dependency that now defines the Fund-Raising Congress. Two changes would make that removal complete. Achieving just one would have made Obama the most important president in a hundred years."

Lessig's twofold recommendations follow. The first is what he calls "citizen-funded elections", possible "in a number of forms"—including a limit of $100 on what each citizen could contribute to political campaigns. The second would be to ban "any member of Congress from working in any lobbying or consulting capacity in Washington for seven years after his or her term."

There is a perfectly simple regulatory act that would . . . [reduce the] influence of money and lobbying in Washington. That would be to ban political advertising.

A Political Auction

Lawrence Lessig's proposals no doubt might make worthy reforms. But Congress has been trying to go straight about funding for almost forty years. Numerous attempts have been made—and some even passed—to limit the amounts of money that can be raised for political campaigns, and the ways in which they can be collected. These efforts, including successive federal electoral-finance statutes, have all focused on the supply-side.

The supply-side has been the characteristic obsession of the Milton Friedmanite [referring to economist Milton Friedman], neo-liberal right since [economist] Arthur Laffer first drew his famous "curve" on a cocktail-napkin. It replaced the characteristic liberal instinct for regulation.

There is a perfectly simple regulatory act that would probably do more than all the supply-side policies in the world to reduce the admittedly unsavoury influence of money and lobbying in Washington. That would be to ban political advertising.

That, after all, is where most of the money raised for political campaigns goes. The work of one scholar, Stephen J. Wayne of Georgetown University, suggests that something like two-thirds of all campaign expenditure goes on advertising, especially TV ads, and another substantial proportion is spent on fund-raising itself. Moreover, TV ads account for a large share of expenditure as the campaign progresses, supporting a presumption that it is decisive in close campaigns.

The emphasis in discussion of campaigning has moved to use of the Internet, for example by Howard Dean in 2004 and by Barack Obama himself in 2008. But the fact is that most money is still spent on paid TV ads, and if they were banned, the cost of campaigns would immediately fall very significantly.

In Britain, however abject its own politicians' concern with their personal finances, political advertising on television is forbidden by law, and the same is true in most other developed democracies.

To most Europeans it would probably seem that paid political advertising, so far from being a palladium of democracy, is actually its opposite. It represents the use of money to resist or withstand public opinion, democratically expressed. The moment the suggestion of banning TV ads is made, the response from anyone familiar with American presidential campaigning is that it could not to be done because it would be *unconstitutional*—contrary to the First Amendment.

What the First Amendment actually says is this: "Congress shall make no law . . . abridging the freedom of speech, or of the press . . ."

The relevance of that very broad text (and I have omitted other clauses referring to freedom of worship and of assembly and petition) is that the Supreme Court (a conservative-dominated court) found in a lawsuit called *Buckley v. Valeo*, that paid television advertising was a form of free speech, and that therefore Congress might not abridge it.

Buckley, it may be noted, was James L. Buckley, the brother of the better-known conservative champion, William F. Buckley Jr., and the candidate of the Conservative Party in New York. (Valeo was an election official attempting to enforce a congressional-campaign finance law.) So while *Buckley v. Valeo* is indeed settled law—and is about to be reinforced by a new court judgment—it is hardly a neutral or apolitical enactment.

A Political Judgment

Now, however, so far from banning or regulating paid political advertising, the American polity has actually reinforced it. The Supreme Court, in a judgment of 21 January 2010 on the case *Citizens United v. Federal Election Commission*, actually narrowed the possibility of regulating political advertising; the probable result will be more campaign spending on TV as "a torrent of attack advertisements from outside groups aiming to sway voters". The National Association of Broadcasters actually quantified the prospective hit at an additional $300 million in ads for the midterm elections in November 2010.

President Obama, a former law professor, immediately understood the political significance of the Court's decision. "The Supreme Court", he said, in uncharacteristically populist language, "has given a green light to a new stampede of special-interest money in our politics. It is a major victory for Big Oil, Wall Street banks, health-insurance companies and the other powerful interests that marshal their power every day in Washington to drown out the voices of everyday Americans."

Some commentators have attempted to argue that the ruling will result in more moderates being elected. That is a very perverse interpretation. The fact is that a very conservative Supreme Court has abandoned any shred of neutrality and delivered a judgment that reinforces the Republican Party at the very moment when President Obama is frustrated at every turn and when the prospect for substantial Republican gains in the 2010 midterm elections look certain.

[The US Supreme Court] has made it less likely than ever that the corruption of American politics can be reversed.

A year ago, many people in the United States, and even more around the world, hoped that Barack Obama's victory would rescue American democracy from a conservative ascendancy that was doing it grave damage in financial and foreign policy and in its contempt for the constitutional tradition and the rule of law.

Now the Court, the institution that in *Bush v. Gore* handed the 2000 election to the people who were to respond so disastrously to the atrocity of 2001 and the financial crisis of 2007–08, has made it less likely than ever that the corruption of American politics can be reversed.

Organizations to Contact

The editors have compiled the following list of organizations concerned with the issues debated in this book. The descriptions are derived from materials provided by the organizations. All have publications or information available for interested readers. The list was compiled on the date of publication of the present volume; names, addresses, phone and fax numbers, and e-mail and Internet addresses may change. Be aware that many organizations take several weeks or longer to respond to inquiries, so allow as much time as possible.

Brookings Institution
1775 Massachusetts Avenue NW, Washington, DC   20036
(202) 797-6000
website: www.brookings.edu

The Brookings Institution is a private, nonprofit research organization that provides analysis and recommendations for policy makers on a wide range of public policy issues. Its website contains information on US politics and campaign finance reform, with links to a number of publications on the topic.

Center for Responsive Politics
1101 Fourteenth Street NW, Suite 1030
Washington, DC   20005-5635
(202) 857-0044 • fax: (202) 857-7809
website: www.opensecrets.org

The Center for Responsive Politics is a nonpartisan, nonprofit research group that tracks money in politics and its effect on elections and public policy. The center conducts computer-based research on campaign finance issues for the news media, academics, activists, and the public at large. Its website contains up-to-date information, charts, and other data on federal election funding, campaign finance, and lobbying in the United States.

Change Congress/Fix Congress First

543 Howard Street, 5th Floor, San Francisco, CA   94105
e-mail: info@change-congress.org
website: www.fixcongressfirst.org

Change Congress is a nonpartisan advocacy organization with a sole purpose of protecting the independence of Congress by fighting the influence of money in politics. FixCongress First.org, a project of Change Congress, seeks to restore public trust in the US government by passing a hybrid of small-dollar donations and public financing of elections. The project was founded by Harvard Law School professor Lawrence Lessig and Joe Trippi, a political strategist who has worked on presidential campaigns for Walter Mondale, Gary Hart, Richard Gephardt, John Edwards, and Howard Dean. The website provides information about the Fair Elections Now Act and a blog featuring many articles and links to articles about government corruption.

Citizens for Responsibility and Ethics
in Washington (CREW)

1400 Eye Street NW, Suite 450, Washington, DC   20005
(202) 408-5565
website: www.citizensforethics.org

Citizens for Responsibility and Ethics in Washington (CREW) is a legal advocacy group that targets corrupt government officials and uses litigation and public advocacy to expose corrupt activities. The CREW website contains information about corruption scandals and the group's various legal actions. Its recent reports include "Most Corrupt Members of Congress" and "Top Ten Ethics Scandals of 2009."

Common Cause

1133 Nineteenth Street NW, 9th floor, Washington, DC   20036
(202) 833-1200
website: www.commoncause.org

Common Cause is a nonpartisan, nonprofit advocacy organization founded in 1970 by John Gardner to encourage citizen participation in democracy and to promote an honest, open, and accountable government. It has almost three hundred thousand members and supporters, with offices in thirty-eight states. Its website contains a wealth of information about money in US politics and anticorruption reforms. Its recent reports include "Campaign Finance Reform: A New Era" and "Taking Elections Off the Auction Block."

Federal Election Commission (FEC)

999 E Street NW, Washington, DC   20463
(800) 424-9530
website: www.fec.gov

The US Congress created the Federal Election Commission as an independent agency in 1975 to administer and enforce the Federal Election Campaign Act (FECA), the statute that governs the financing of federal elections. The duties of the FEC are to disclose campaign finance information, to enforce the provisions of the law such as the limits and prohibitions on contributions, and to oversee the public funding of presidential elections. The FEC website provides information about campaign finance laws, recent developments in the law, and enforcement efforts.

Pew Research Center

1615 L Street NW, Suite 700, Washington, DC   20036
(202) 419-4300 • fax: (202) 419-4349
website: http://pewresearch.org

The Pew Research Center is a nonpartisan "fact tank" that provides information on the issues, attitudes, and trends shaping America and the world. It conducts public opinion polls and social science research, reports and analyzes news, and holds forums and briefings, but it does not take positions on policy issues. A search of the center's website produces publications on the public's views on the financial crisis, health care reform, and government corruption.

Project On Government Oversight (POGO)

1100 G Street NW, Suite 900, Washington, DC   20005-3806

(202) 347-1122 • fax: (202) 347-1116
e-mail: info@pogo.org
website: www.pogo.org

Founded in 1981, the Project On Government Oversight (POGO) is a nonpartisan, independent watchdog that champions government reforms. POGO's mission is to investigate corruption, misconduct, and conflicts of interest to achieve a more effective, accountable, open, and ethical federal government. The group's website contains a publications library that provides access to books, reports, and newsletters on the subject of government conduct and reform.

Transparency International—USA (TI-USA)
1023 Fifteenth Street NW, Suite 300, Washington, DC 20005
(202) 589-1616 • fax: (202) 589-1512
website: www.transparency-usa.org

Transparency International (TI) is a Berlin-based nonprofit, nonpartisan organization founded in 1993 to curb corruption in international trade and transactions. TI has chapters in more than eighty countries, including the United States. It encourages governments to implement effective anticorruption laws and policies, promotes reform through international organizations, and raises public awareness. Its USA website contains a link to the main TI website as well as a long list of publications on the topic of corruption.

Bibliography

Books

Ravi Batra	*The New Golden Age: The Coming Revolution Against Political Corruption and Economic Chaos.* New York: Palgrave, 2007.
Toby J.F. Bishop and Frank E. Hydoski	*Corporate Resiliency: Managing the Growing Risk of Fraud and Corruption.* Hoboken, NJ: Wiley, 2009.
Elizabeth Drew	*The Corruption of American Politics: What Went Wrong and Why.* Secaucus, NJ: Carol Publishing Group, 1999.
Richard Duncan	*The Corruption of Capitalism: A Strategy to Rebalance the Global Economy and Restore Sustainable Growth.* Hong Kong: CLSA Books, 2009.
Michael A. Genovese and Victoria A. Farrar-Myers, eds.	*Corruption and American Politics.* Amherst, NY: Cambria Press, 2010.
Edward L. Glaeser and Claudia Goldin, eds.	*Corruption and Reform: Lessons from America's Economic History.* Chicago: University of Chicago Press, 2006.

Mark Green — *Selling Out: How Big Corporate Money Buys Elections, Rams Through Legislation, and Betrays Our Democracy*. New York: HarperCollins, 2002.

Mark Grossman — *Political Corruption in America: An Encyclopedia of Scandals, Power, and Greed*. Millerton, NY: Grey House Publishing, 2008.

Jim Hightower — *Thieves in High Places: They've Stolen Our Country—and It's Time to Take It Back*. New York: Viking, 2003.

Kurt Hohenstein — *Coining Corruption: The Making of the American Campaign Finance System*. Dekalb, IL: Northern Illinois University Press, 2007.

Arianna Huffington — *Pigs at the Trough: How Corporate Greed and Political Corruption Are Undermining America*. New York: Three Rivers Press, 2009.

Robert G. Kaiser — *So Damn Much Money: The Triumph of Lobbying and the Corrosion of American Government*. New York: Vintage Books, 2010.

Robert Kuttner — *A Presidency in Peril: The Inside Story of Obama's Promise, Wall Street's Power, and the Struggle to Control Our Economic Future*. White River Junction, VT: Chelsea Green Publishing, 2010.

Kim Long	*The Almanac of Political Corruption, Scandals, and Dirty Politics.* New York: Delacorte Press, 2007.
Nancy E. Marion	*The Politics of Disgrace: The Role of Political Scandal in American Politics.* Durham, NC: Carolina Academic Press, 2009.
Peter H. Stone	*Casino Jack and the United States of Money: Superlobbyist Jack Abramoff and the Buying of Washington.* Brooklyn, NY: Melville House, 2010.

Periodicals and Internet Sources

David A. Andelman	"The World's Most Corrupt Countries," *Forbes*, April 3, 2007. www.forbes.com.
Belfast Telegraph	"US Wakes Up to Scale of Financial Corruption," May 14, 2010. www.belfasttelegraph.co.uk.
David Brooks	"Don't Follow the Money," *New York Times*, October 18, 2010. www.nytimes.com.
Loren Cobb	"Corruption in America," *Quaker Economist*, May 27, 2007. www.quaker.org.
Terry Easton	"10 Steps to Fix the U.S. Financial Crisis," *Human Events*, February 20, 2010. www.humanevents.com.

The Economic Collapse (blog)	"The Unbelievably Rampant Corruption on Wall Street," 2010. TheEconomicCollapseBlog.com.
Economist	"The Usual Suspects," October 26, 2010. www.economist.com.
Chris Edwards	"Transparency and Control: Improving Financial Management in Congress," Cato Institute, May 25, 2006. www.cato.org.
William Fisher	"US Slides on Corruption Index," Inter Press Service, October 29, 2010. Ipsnorthamerica.net.
Tom Fitton	"Judicial Watch Announces List of Washington's 'Ten Most Wanted Corrupt Politicians' for 2009," *Judical Watch*, January 1, 2010.
Michael Grunwald	"Financial Reform: Obama's Triumph of Policy over Politics," *Time*, July 21, 2010. www.time.com.
William M. Isaac	"Obama's Financial Reform Weak and Ineffective," *Forbes*, April 22, 2010. www.forbes.com.
Samuel Issacharoff	"On Political Corruption," NYU School of Law, Public Law Research Paper No. 10–54, August 19, 2010. Papers.ssrn.com.
David D. Kirkpatrick	"Does Corporate Money Lead to Political Corruption?" *New York Times*, January 23, 2010. www.nytimes.com.

Joshua Matz   "*Citizens United*: What Happens Next?" *Harvard Law Record*, February 11, 2010. www.hlrecord.org.

New York Times   "Financial Regulatory Reform," November 4, 2010. Topics.nytimes.com.

Rick Schmitt   "Prophet and Loss," *Stanford Magazine*, March–April 2009. www.stanfordalumni.org.

Steve Simpson   "*Citizens United* and the Battle for Free Speech in America," *Objective Standard*, Spring 2010. www.theobjectivestandard.com.

Chad Terhune and Keith Epstein   "The Health Insurers Have Already Won," *BusinessWeek*, August 6, 2009. www.businessweek.com.

Index